PULBOROUGH
A Pictorial History

PULBOROUGH

A Pictorial History

Ivy Linda Strudwick

PHILLIMORE

1983

Published by
PHILLIMORE & CO. LTD.
Shopwyke Hall, Chichester, Sussex

ISBN 0 85033 493 4

Printed and bound in Great Britain by
BILLING & SONS LIMITED
Guildford, London, Oxford, Worcester

CONTENTS

List of Illustrations

Acknowledgements

I   The Domesday entry for Pulborough

II   Ordnance Survey Map of Pulborough

III   Pulborough

IV   St. Mary's Church

V   The Rectory

VI   Schools—old and new

VII   Village Hall and carnivals

VIII   Life as a shop assistant at Oliver's Stores in the 1920s

IX   Changes in Pulborough

X   Postal history

XI   Bus service

XII   Women's Institute

XIII   Historic houses and bridges

XIV   Clubs, Societies and Associations

I dedicate this book
to the memory of my dear husband, Clifford,
who loved Pulborough where he lived all his life.
He was always very happy to
reminisce about the olden days.

LIST OF ILLUSTRATIONS

1. Church Hill, 1907
2. Swan Corner, 1907
3. Floods at Swan Bridge, 1907
4. View from the *Arun Hotel*, 1906
5. The Railway Station entrance
6. Sailing barge, 1898
7. Map of the Arun and Wey Canal
8. Hardham Tunnel
9. Extensive flooding, 1968
10. Aerial view, 1971
11. Aerial view, 1972
12. Wickford Bridge
13. St Mary's church, from the N.E., 1791
14. St Mary's church tower
15. Bellringers of the past
16. A later photograph of the bellringers
17. Centre aisle and chancel, St Mary's church, 1908
18. Pulborough church choir, c.1915
19. The 12th-century font, St Mary's church
19a. Lovely oak screen, St Mary's church
20. Pulborough Church Lad's Brigade, 1908
21. Institution and induction of Rev. St C. A. Maltin
22. St Mary's church organ, 1980
23. The United Reform church
24. The Roman Catholic church
25. St Botolph's church, Hardham
26. Stopham church
27. Wiggonholt church
28. Rev. William Sinclair and family
29. The old Rectory
30. 'Old Walls'
31. The present day Rectory
32. Almshouses after modernisation
33. The Glebe Barn
34. Pulborough old school and Master's house
35. Pupils at Pulborough school, 1888
36. Teachers and Pupils, 1904
37. After the old school was altered
38. North Heath school
39. Nutbourne school
40. Pulborough's new primary school
41. The primary school swimming pool
42. May Revels, 1920s
43. The Village Hall, 1932
44. Interior of the Village Hall, 1932
45 The first Carnival procession, 1931
46. The same procession arriving at the Village Hall
47. Carnival procession, 1934
48. Float in the Whit-Monday Carnival, 1935
49. Children's party at the Village Hall, 1937
50. Victory Revels procession, 1946
51. Float in the Carnival, 1946
52. Fire-walking 'Lenz' at the Victory Revels
53. Victory Revels Queen on her way to the Village Hall
54. The crowning of the Victory Revels Queen
55. Carnival procession
56. Wilfred and Mabel Pickles at the Village Hall
57. Chanctonbury Lions' Dinner, 1948
58. The Village Hall committee, 1957
59. The author, 1957
60. Oliver's Stores, 1922
61. Chelsea Pensioners outside Oliver's Stores, 1954
62. The interior of Oliver's Stores
63. The last of six cottages demolished to make way for Allfrey Plat
64. Allfrey Plat
65. Three old cottages in Lower Street
66. Heron Rye
67. Cecil Strudwick's cycle shop
68. Killick's house shop and bakehouses
69. The Doctor's surgeries
70. Tribe's butcher's shop and house
71. Miss Gardener's Cottage
71a. Detail from No. 71
72. The *Swan Hotel* and Corn Exchange
72a. Detail from No. 72
73. The *Arun Hotel*
74. The *Water's Edge Hotel*
75. The *Chequers Hotel*
76. After the *Chequers Hotel* Fire, 1963
77. The 15th-century chapel at the rear of the *Chequers Hotel*
78. The *Red Lion*
79. The *Five Bells*
80. Ruins of the *Rose and Crown*
81. The *White Horse*
82. The *White Hart*
83. The *Oddfellows*
83a. Sales Cottage, 1908
84. 'Le-Bijou, Mare Hill Road
85. 'Yeomans', Mare Hill

86. The Post Office before 1906
87. The Post Office, 1907
88. Royal Mail van at Storrington, 1911
89. Henley's barn, Lower Street
90. Postal uniforms through the ages
91. Letter box at Little Bognor
92. Letter box at Bignor
93. Letter box at Wiggonholt
94. Letter box at Pulborough station
95. The first No. 1 bus
96. No. 1 bus filling up with passengers
97. Southdown bus, 1948
98. Women's Institute drama group, 1956
99. Women's Institute; Miss Malcolm planting a tree
100. Women's Institute members, 1970
101. Denman College
102. Women's Institute Diamond Jubilee, 1978
103. Outing to Wilton House, 1972
104. Old Place
105. Mill Cottage
106. New Place Manor
107. The famous gateway at New Place Manor
108. Dovecote at New Place Manor
109. New Place Manor chimney
110. Coombelands
111. Hardham Priory
112. Stopham House
113. Stopham Bridge
114. Jubilee Bridge at Stopham
115. Puttocks Farm
116. The Old Cottage, Church Hill, 1909
116a. Detail of No. 116
117. Old Timbers and Horncroft
118. Corden's Chemist shop
119. Detail of 118
120. The corn stores
121. H. Fielder's shop
122. Demolition of H. Fielder's shop
123. Lloyds bank
124. Pulborough House
125. Wharfe House
126. Tudor Park Farm
127. Henley's, Lower Street
128. Chilham House
129. Hardham Mill and house
130. The West Sussex Southern Water Authority Works, Hardham
131. Enlargement work at the Water Works
132. Beedings
133. Toat Monument
134. Clements bridge
135. Clements bridge and the railway bridge
136. Old and new Swan bridges
137. Dedication of the Red Cross Bed, 1939
138. Red Cross inspection, 1939
139. The ambulance station
140. A posted photograph of the Ambulance men
141. St John's cadets, 1926
142. St John's, 1947
143. St John's members, 1948
144. Mr. L. Atfield at Hastings, 1964
145. St John's new ambulance
146. Dedication of the Royal British Legion's first standard
147. Armistice Sunday service, c.1942
148. Dedication of the Royal British Legion's new standard
149. Mr. Arthur Woods with the new standard
150. Pulborough Bowling Club, 1922
151. Bowling Club members, 1956
152. Bowling Club dinner, c.1956
153. Codmore Hill Cricket Club, 1913
154. Butler's tea sloshers
155. Present day Cricket Club, 1980
156. The Men's Club, Lower Street
157. Stoolball Club
158. Football Club, the 'Red Robins'
159. Football team, 1980
160. Rugby team, 1980
161. Pulborough Scouts
162. Scouts parading along Lower Street
163. Pulborough Cubs
164. Jumble sale helpers
165. The new Youth Headquarters

ACKNOWLEDGEMENTS

A long time ago I started collecting photographs of Pulborough. About five years ago, prompted by the general disappearance of the old village, the idea came to me to put on record a few of these changes before they are lost forever.

I am most grateful to many friends who kindly lent me photographs to add to my fine collection, also books from which I have been able to gain extra knowledge of the village in the past.

I should like to thank the following for giving me permission to use articles, photographs and maps: *West Sussex Gazette*; *Worthing Gazette*; *Motor Boat* and *Yachting*; Southdown Motor Services; Horsham District Council; National Federation of Women's Institutes Books Ltd; Mr. P. D. Churchill; Jenwood Features; Aerofilms Limited; Mr. J. Armour-Milne; Head Post Office, Worthing; Letter Box Study Group; Postal Headquarters, London; Mrs. P. Gill, B.A., Archivist, Record Office, Chichester; and the Southern Water Authority.

Rotbř ten de com̅ POLEBERGE . Vluric̃ tenuit . T . R . E .
Tc̅ 7 m̅ fe defđ p . xvi . hiđ . Tra . e̅ . xviii . cař . In dn̅io
funt . iiii . cař . 7 xxxv . uitti 7 xv . cot cu̅ xiii . cař .
Ibi . ix . ferui . 7 ii . molini de . xi . fot . 7 xxx . ac̅ p̅ti . 7 filua:
de . xxv . porc̃ . 7 ii . pifcariæ de . iii . fot . Ibi . ii . æcclæ .
De t̅ra huj M̅ ten Tetbald 7 Iuo . ii . hiđ 7 dim virga̅ .
7 ibi in dn̅io . i . cař . 7 iii . uitti 7 iiii . cot cu̅ . i . cař .
Totu̅ M̅ T . R . E . uatb . xvi . lib . 7 poft: xvi . lib . Modo:
dn̅ium Rotti: xxii . lib . Hominu̅: xxxv . fot .

Robert holds PULBOROUGH from the Earl. Wulfric held it
before 1066. Then and now it answered for 16 hides.
Land for 18 ploughs. In lordship 4 ploughs;
  35 villagers and 15 cottagers with 13 ploughs.
  9 slaves; 2 mills at 11s; meadow, 30 acres; woodland at 25 pigs;
    2 fisheries at 3s. 2 churches.
  Theobald and Ivo hold 2 hides and ½ virgate of this
    manor's land. In lordship 1 plough;
  3 villagers and 4 cottagers with 1 plough.
Value of the whole manor before 1066 £16; later £16;
now, Robert's lordship £22; the mens' 35s.

1 The Domesday Entry for Pulborough

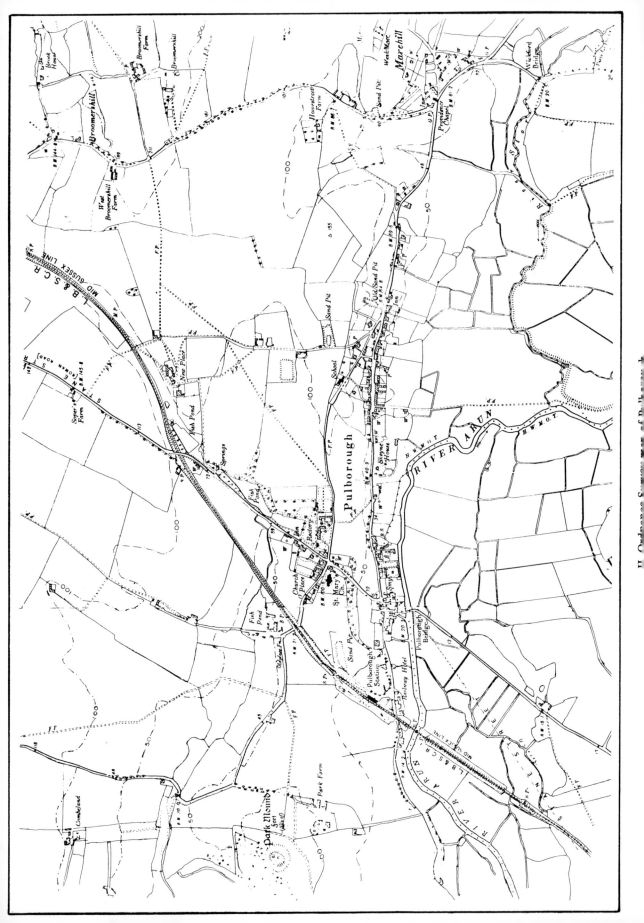

II. Ordnance Survey Map of Pulborough

III PULBOROUGH

The name Pulborough was first mentioned in Domesday Book and is derived from the Welsh 'Pwll', a pool, and as being an earth-work.

It is an extensive village parish, 46 miles from London. The great Roman road, Stane Street, from Regnum to Londinium passed through Pulborough in a direct line for a distance of three and a half miles, and near it many indications of Roman occupations have been found. There is no circumstantial evidence to show how Stane Street crossed the Arun marshes from Hardham to Pulborough bridge. No indications of the actual road remain, it probably ran in a direct line along the old ridge to the modern causeway. At the south end, west of the modern road, Roman debris of a house or houses was found. The Roman bridge was thought to be slightly to the east of the present old one, as the foundations of an old bridge abutment were found. Thence the road ran up Church Hill (north-north-east), the present deep cutting in the sand stone. The modern road is in a line with the old Roman Road as far as where three cottages used to stand on the left. The modern road curves to the east to cross the railway bridge, but Stane Street continued straight on behind the cottages and coincided with the modern road again northward from the west end of the bridge. With the exception of a few slight curves the modern road appears to take the same course as Stane Street on to Todhurst Farm and Billingshurst.

Pulborough was once a Gibraltar guarding Stane Street for Rome. The fort was on a mound west of the railway corresponding with the church on the east. Here, probably, was a catapulta and certainly a vigilant garrison, but for many years the only invader was the floods which, most winters, transformed the green waste to the south into a silver sea of which Pulborough was the northern shore and Amberley the southern.

Extensive work has been carried out in late years to build up the banks of the river, but after heavy rain the water still continues to pour over with a mighty roar. Until 1854 trading was carried out with barges which travelled up and down the river, then known as the Wey and Arun Canal, from Littlehampton to London. This canal was dug between 1789 and 1816. Barges laden with coal, chalk, lime, sand and timber were regularly passing under Stopham bridge; by 1822 the annual freightage carried on the canal reached 20,000 tons. By this time the low centre arch was proving a serious impediment to river traffic. In 1822 the Arun Navigation Company made the only major alteration to the bridge in its long history, raising and widening the arch to its present segmental form at a cost of £286.

I understand that a lot of smuggling went on in the olden days. The *Orange Tree* at the top of Monkey Hill, which was then a beer house, was one of the places involved; no doubt there were many others. There were several underground tunnels around Pulborough which could have been used for this purpose.

Barges were no longer needed once the railway line was opened. It was not until the 1930s that the final Closure Acts for the Canals were made law. There was great jubilation when the Horsham to Pulborough railway line was begun in the glebeland near

Pulborough Parish church in December 1857. Many spectators were present, including the directors of the line and several of the local gentry, Mr. Hawkins, traffic manager of the London-Brighton and South Coast Line, and several other officials of the Company. Mr. McCormac, the contractor for the construction of the line, was also present. From the top of the church tower the Union Jack was flying and the bells were ringing out their music when, at about half past one, the ceremony began with a short prayer by the Rev. Sinclair, rector of the parish. Captain Bartelott of Stopham then dug the first sod and having tossed it into a wheelbarrow it was wheeled away amid the cheering of the spectators. The weather was anything but favourable. The line was completed and opened in 1863.

There have been several excavations of Roman villas in the past years, one at Borough Farm in 1909. This is thought to be the earliest villa in Sussex; certainly the earliest one north of the Downs unless there was an earlier structure at Bignor. A Roman site, a posting station, was discovered in 1926 at Hardham.

At Holmstreet Farm, in 1910, Roman walls were found, but there is no Roman significance in 'Street'. Holmstreet was formerly Holmstreke (1485) meaning Holly Strip. About half a mile west of this and a good furlong north of the Pulborough-Wiggonholt road, in 1900, a small rectangular building thought to be a temple, was excavated; and there was probably a Roman building in Pulborough churchyard. In 1929 heavy pieces of Roman flanged roof tiles were dug out in the making of graves. There is a little collection of Roman objects, which were in the church for many years, at the new Church of England (aided) Primary School.

Wickford Bridge at the south-easterly part of the village is built on a sharp bend and crosses the river Stor. This road connects Pulborough with Wiggonholt and Storrington. On the left after leaving the bridge (the road has since been altered), the site of a Roman bath house has been revealed. In the 1700s there was a mill near the south end of Mill Lane. A road went down between Bookers (now No. 147A Lower Street) and No. 1 Rivermead and continued on, turning left at the bottom to the mill. This road is now partly filled in and the rest just a ditch with high banks each side. The Mill Lane houses were built in 1938.

1. The Old Cottage at the top of Church Hill, 1907.

2. Swan Corner, 1907. From a watercolour by C. Essenhigh Corre.

3. (*below*) Flooding at Swan Bridge, 1907.

4. (*opposite above*) View of Lower Street from the top of the *Arun Hotel*, 1906.

5. (*opposite below*) The front entrance of the Railway Station, built in 1859.

Railway Station, Pulborough

6. One of the last sailing barges to be used on the River Arun in 1898, owned by Mr. Harry Doick (centre). With him are his sons Percy and Tom.

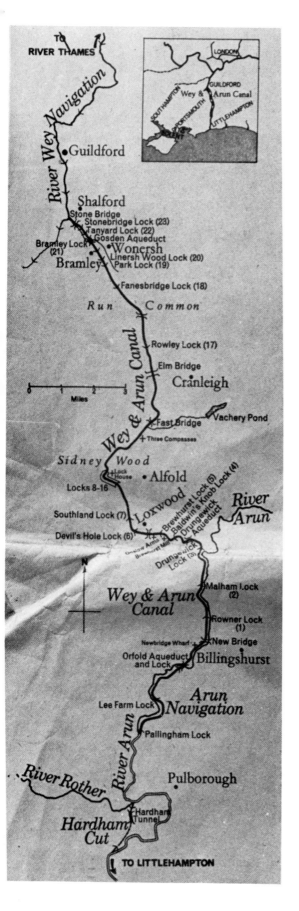

7. Map of the Arun and Wey Canal, showing 23 locks.

8. Hardham Tunnel used in the days of barges. The men would lie on their backs in the barge and kick their way through on the roof of the tunnel, while the horses went overland.

9. View of extensive flooding which occurred on 16 September 1968.

10. Aerial view from the eastern end of Pulborough, March 1971.

11. Aerial view of Pulborough, December 1972.

12. Wickford Bridge at the south-easterly end of the village built on a sharp bend over the River Stor.

IV ST. MARY'S CHURCH

In any village the main building should be the church, and in Pulborough we have a very beautiful one dedicated to St. Mary or Our Lady of the Assumption.

It is constructed principally of local sandstone with a Horsham stone tiled roof. It consists of nave, aisles, north and south porches, chancel, vestry and western embattled tower, which is a prominent landmark from the surrounding countryside, and contains a clock and a peal of eight bells. The oldest bell was cast in 1500 and the latest are three bells cast to commemorate Queen Victoria's Jubilee in 1897. The bells are rung every Sunday by a loyal and enthusiastic band of ringers, which has included a member of the Corden family since 1887.

The oldest part of the church is the chancel built c.1180; the nave and aisles were added in the early 15th century. Until 1958 the organ was housed in what is now the Olney Chapel and it was one of the kind which had to be pumped by hand. The choir stalls were also in the chancel, and until 1944 there was always a full choir to lead the singing with as many as 25 members or more.

When the church was first built it would seat 500 persons, but the building of the new organ necessitated losing many seats. The High Altar, as I knew it for many years, was taken out and replaced with the present one in 1950.

There are various memorial slabs and two ancient brasses besides many inscriptions to the Apsley, Coles, Legg, Spragg, Marriott, Cobb and Trendcroft families. The east window and others are also memorials.

Church registers date from the year 1595. I am not able to give all the names of the past Rectors, but our present Rector, Rev. Basil St. C. A. Maltin, is the 39th. The five previous Rectors were: Rev. Sinclair, 1857-1878; Rev. Burke, 1878-1904; Canon Baggaley, 1904-1921; Rev. Frost, 1921-1944; Rev. Royle, 1944-1970.

Until 1939 there was an Assistant Curate and his house was Hillside in the London Road, on the left just after leaving the church; it was dedicated by the Venerable Archdeacon of Chichester on 7 November 1927. The house then became the home of the Organist-Choirmaster. We had some excellent Organist-Choirmasters in the past who trained the choir to perform some wonderful works. My husband Clifford was a member from the age of eight until the age of 52 years and was the last remaining male member when the choir was transferred to the back of the church. Singing was part of his life, he sang bass and tenor solos in 'The Crucifixion' by J. Stainer a total of 17 times.

The original choir vestry has now become the Rector's vestry. The choir stalls were in the chancel and it was usual for the choir to process and recess singing a hymn. In those days they were expected to lead the singing. Dr. White was the Organist-Choirmaster for several years before leaving for America in 1950. During his time here we had a special treat. Sir Adrian Boult, a friend of Dr. White, brought his string orchestra to Pulborough church and made it possible for us to listen to a wonderful musical evening.

The dedication of the church organ was by the Lord Bishop of Chichester on Ascension Day, Tuesday 15 May 1947 at 8 p.m. After the service the Rev. W. C. M. Cochrane, M.A.,

Mus.B., A.R.C.O., Director of Music at Christ's Hospital, gave a recital. The organ was formerly the property of Charles Mortimer, Esq., J.P. and was built for his house, Wigmore, at Holmwood, Surrey by Bryceson Bros., in 1895. No expense seems to have been spared in the design and equipment of this organ which is a magnificent example of the organ builder's craft. The organ was re-erected in the church by the John Compton Organ Company Limited. There are nearly 1,800 pipes in the organ.

In addition to the parish church of St. Mary, there are three other most interesting churches quite near. These are all much smaller; at Hardham, Stopham and Wiggonholt.

Some interesting 19th-century church events are worth a mention. The following have been taken from past Sussex publications:

3rd May, 1850—Re-opening of Pulborough Church

'Wednesday last was observed as a day of rejoicing in the Parish of Pulborough on account of the re-opening of the noble old Parish Church which had been closed for some months for restoration and repair. Unsightly galleries, in most of which it was impossible to see or hear, were taken down; high square pews, in the old churchwarden style, were removed and a monster pulpit which, with a curious revolving reading desk, completely shut out the spacious chancel was replaced by a handsome pulpit and desk of oak. The whole chancel, nave and aisles are now fitted up with neat open seats, affording more accommodation than was provided by the former comfortless arrangement and a stained glass window has been put up at the east end of the chancel in memory of the late Rev. J. Austin as a record and acknowledgement of his liberal bequest of £3,000 to promote education in the parish, and the glass for another painted window was presented by the Rev. W. Gore of Rusper and the stone work by Mr. G. M. Hills of John Street, Adelphi, the able architect, who has superintended the restoration. The congregation assembled at half past eleven, the Rector read prayers and the new organ was played by a lady of the congregation. The sermon was preached by the Rector's brother, the Venerable Archdeacon of Middlesex, on Matthew ch. 6, verse 9 'Hallowed be thy name'.

There was evening service at 6 o'clock, after the service the ringers were entertained at supper given by Mr. and Mrs. Sinclair at the Rectory and we hope that the fine old peal of bells will now be rung regularly on Sundays and suitable occasions and thus enliven the parish far and near.'

2nd August, 1862—Pulborough Church Choir

'On the 24th ultimo the members of the above choir, numbering about 25, went on their annual trip, this time it was determined to take them to Brighton. Accordingly, about 6.30 a.m. they started from Pulborough accompanied by the Curates, the Rev. J. Knight and P. Royston. A Fly and pair and a van and pair took the happy party to Steyning whence they proceeded by rail to Brighton. The Rector, the Rev. W. Sinclair, kindly supplied the party with refreshments for the day. After spending eight hours by the seaside and enjoying themselves as much as possible they returned to Pulborough arriving at 8.30 p.m., highly gratified with their trip and grateful to their benefactors who took so much interest in their welfare.'

6th October, 1868—Pulborough Choir Treat

'On Saturday, the 26th ultimo, the children of the three choirs of Pulborough, North Heath and Nutbourne were taken in a barge party to Amberley. The Rev. G. Cavill and Mrs. Cavill, W. M. Sinclair, Esq., and Miss Sinclair, Rev. Allen, Mr. and Mrs. Allen, Mrs. Bishop, Miss Bolton, Miss B. Byram, etc. accompanied the party. The day was pleasantly spent among the interesting ruins which the Rev. G. A. Clarkson, the Vicar, was good enough to explain. A plentiful dinner and tea were demolished under the shade of the castle walnut trees. The choirs have already visited the Crystal Palace, Portsmouth Dockyards, the Zoological Gardens in Regents Park, Brighton, Arundel, etc., it is hoped next year to take them to Chichester Cathedral; Mr. W. Dean of Chichester Cathedral has undertaken the tuition of the Pulborough choir and it is proposed to join it to the Chichester Choral Association in the coming year.'

13. View from the north-east, from a
drawing by S. H. Grimm, 1791.

14. St Mary's Tower from the west.

15. Bellringers of the past; among them are Messrs. Corden, Goodsell, Smart, Greenfield, Dalmon, Knight, Wadey, Booker, Doick and Stone.

16. A later photograph of bellringers,—Messrs. Greenfield, Corden, Killick, Orford, Doick, Goodsell, Knight and Gorden

17. Centre aisle and chancel of St Mary's church, 1908. Note the absence of iron railings at the entrance to the chancel.

18. Pulborough church choir *c*.1915, with Canon Baggaley in the centre.

19. This 12th-century font of Purbeck marble on a modern sandstone base is thought to have come from an earlier church.

19a. The lovely oak screen by Sir Ninian Comper, at the west end of the nave. The steps on the far side lead to the tower.

20.   Pulborough Church Lads' Brigade, 1908, including such names as,—Goodsell, Smith, Humphry, Wadey, Pannel, Wilson Baggaley, Canon Baggaley, Corden, Elliott and Sandilands.

21. (*below left*) The Institution and induction of our present rector, Rev. Basil St C. A. Maltin, took place on 16 January 1971. He is the 39th in succession to Thomas Harlying, 1402-3; the sixth to be appointed to the living in 114 years. Left to right are the Rev. Owen Q. Haigh, Rural Dean; the Venerable Lancelot Mason, Archdeacon; Rev. Basil Maltin; the Right Rev. Dr. Roger Wilson, Bishop of Chichester; and Rev. Alec MacDonald, who acted as Bishop's Chaplain.

22. (*below right*) In September 1980 an appeal was launched to raise £1,000 to thoroughly overhaul the church organ.

23. The United Reform church at the east end of the village in Lower Street which replaced the old Congregational chapel at Mare Hill.

24. The Roman Catholic church, in Church Place, is dedicated to St Crispin and St Crispinian.

25. St Botolph's at Hardham which dates from the 11th century and contains perhaps the earliest complete series of mural paintings in England. The little church, which has every right to call itself the oldest picture gallery in England, should not be missed by any visitor to Pulborough.

26. Stopham has a lovely little church dating from the 14th century, filled with a magnificent series of brasses and memorials to the Bartelott family which held lands here from the 11th century. Their ancient manor house is situated near the confluence of the Rother and the Arun.

27. Wiggonholt church. This little church has no patron saint and was built for the use of the shepherds who worked in the Brook. The original walls are 12th or 13th century and most of the windows are in the Perpendicular style (1360-1485). The stained glass east window was made by Powell & Sons in 1859. The Sussex marble font is late Norman. The remaining parts of the Jacobean rails are now in the nave and two old sundials, or clocks, for showing the times of the service may be found on the south-west corner of the outside of the church. Records of rectors and curates are known from 1422 the parish records for baptisms go back to 1510.

V THE RECTORY

The beautiful Queen Anne Rectory, which stands on high ground near the church overlooking the Brooks and South Downs, was built and paid for by the Rev. Francis Mose, rector of the parish from 1720-1729. It was then given to the parish for the use of his successors. During the reign of Queen Victoria another storey was added by the Rev. Sinclair, presumably to house his large family and servants. During my young days when Canon Baggaley and the Rev. Frost were in residence they kept a staff of five servants, three gardeners and a chauffeur. The two houses, one on the right as you turn in towards the Rectory opposite the *Chequers* Hotel, and the one which has been enlarged, past the Rectory on the left, now named 'Old Walls', were both gardeners' cottages. The grounds extended to the road which leads up to New Place Manor. There was a lovely lake with a punt on it and it was possible to walk all round the lake. When the chestnuts were ready, the children were allowed to go after Sunday School and pick up as many as we liked; these we took home, roasted and enjoyed.

The top storey of the Rectory was later removed, so the house today looks very much as it was when it was first built. In 1973 the Diocesan Dilapidations Board wanted to sell the building and replace it with a smaller, modern house but, because the Rectory had become such a general meeting place for the Parish, I thought it would be a shame for this to happen. In April 1973 I started a petition to save our beautiful Rectory for future generations to enjoy and, with Mrs. Henderson's and other's help, we collected 1,059 signatures. I am very pleased to say we saved the building.

In October 1974 workmen moved in to carry out internal alterations and improvements, to restore the building and convert the east wing, once the old kitchens, etc., into Parish rooms. Now the living quarters are entirely separate from the Parish rooms and there is a new modern kitchen in the west wing. It was all right in the olden days to have such a rambling place; there were plenty of servants to do the fetching and carrying and to negotiate a steep flight of steps from the dining room down to the kitchen. The new Parish rooms have made an ideal centre for the children in the Sunday School who formerly met in the Rectory itself.

We will now travel back along the road to what were the Almshouses, built in 1862 by the generosity of Mrs. Ann Burrell, with an income of £12 yearly and used for the needy of the Parish. They are now converted into homes for retired priests and their wives, or the widows of priests.

There is a fine War Memorial which stands between these houses and the flight of steps up to the church.

28. This photograph is believed to be of the Rev. William Sinclair and family.

29. The Old Rectory, date unknown.

30. 'Old Walls', which has since been extended, was once a gardener's cottage.

1. The Rectory as it is today.

32. Almshouses, now modernised and used as homes for retired priests and their wives, or widows.

33. The lovely old barn between the Rectory and 'Old Walls', converted into an attractive house in 1951-52. Note the dovecote which is about thirty yards from the house.

VI SCHOOLS OLD AND NEW

Background history of Pulborough Parish Schools

The Rev. John Austin, Rector of Pulborough, who died on 4 December 1856, left by will over £3,000 'for the promotion of education in Pulborough Parish of certain poor children in useful learning and arts'.

Up to that time the only school that existed was a little one-storey building on Pot Common, not far from the present school. A writer in one of the Women's Institute Records has written, 'In 1855 no fewer than four schools of varying types are listed in the Post Office Directory for Sussex. One of these was a boarding school in Pot Street, Pulborough, run by a Thomas Lucas'. Nothing is remembered of these schools now; they were probably small Dame schools at which a few pupils learned to read and write and a little more. Before this date only a few public elementary schools had been built in the County.

The late Miss Baker, who lived in Pulborough nearly all her life and was headmistress of Nutbourne C. of E. School for many years, said of the schools of the parish, 'When the Rev. William Sinclair came to Pulborough in 1857 to succeed the Rev. Austin he at once set to work to carry on the building of schools in Pulborough and also at North Heath and Nutbourne, in the Pulborough Parish—the idea being that the two last schools should be used for Sunday Services as well'.

From the Rev. Austin's bequest £250 was appropriated for the building of Pulborough School and a sum equal to a quarter of the cost went towards the building of the school at North Heath. A grant was also made towards the building of Nutbourne school but how much is not stated. The residue of the money formed a fund, now known as the Austin Trust, for the maintenance of the schools. Income derived from the Trust is still used for the upkeep of the buildings.

Throughout its history Pulborough school has belonged to the Church of England, except for a short period of nine years from the 24 April 1894 when the school was transferred to a locally-elected School Board of five members. The Rector at that time, the Rev. Bourke, was elected Chairman of the Board, Louis Nicholas Corden, clerk to the Board, William Hollman, attendance officer. However, it is evident from correspondence, now in the Chichester archives, that the Rector was not happy about the transfer and in 1903, as a result of his efforts, the Church resumed possession of the school. He died the same day.

The following extracts are from an old school record:

'The site of the National School known as Pot Common was given by the Lords of the Manor, Pulborough, Messrs Dalbiac of Hyde Park, London, in July 1857 for the education of children and adults or children only of the labouring, manufacturing, and other poorer classes of the village and the principal officiating minister, for the time being, was to superintend the religious and moral instruction of the scholars. He could also used the building as a Sunday School.'

'A committee of eight was to administer the school and the first names were those of John Jupp of Broomers Hill, Thomas Jupp of Pythingdean, Henry Comper of Oak House, John Boxall of Park Farm, Thomas Peachey of Old Place and William Heath of New Place, all of them farmers; Peter John Martin, surgeon, and William Taylor, Doctor of medicine, all were to contribute 20 shillings a year to school funds and all to sign a declaration that they were members of the Church of England and Ireland "as by law established". The headmaster and any other staff also had to be members of the Church of England.'

'In April each year the committee was to elect six ladies (also church members) to help in visiting and managing the girl pupils.'

'The new National School was built with stone brought from the quarries at Pythingdean, three miles from the village, and carried in wagon loads by the farmers and, at the end of July, 1857, the pretty village of Pulborough was all astir on the occasion of the laying of the first stone. The shops were closed and all the people made holiday. At half past eleven a.m. the inhabitants assembled at the Church and marched in procession, with banners flying, headed by the Arundel Brass Band to the site of the proposed school. The Rev. William Sinclair, the Rector of the parish, offered up an appropriate series of collects and prayers, after which the first stone was laid by Mrs. Bartelott of Stopham House. The Bartelott family being among the principal contributors to the good work. After the address the National Anthem was sung and three cheers having been given for Mrs. Bartelott and the Rector the assembly marched back to the Rectory where buns were distributed among the children who enjoyed themselves thoroughly, as only children know how. The subscribers and principal parishioners partook of luncheon in a neat marquee upon the lawn of the Rectory. The event was celebrated by the villagers by a cricket match in a field lent by the Rector for the purpose—the married against the single. Afterwards both the victorious and the vanquished sat down to an excellent dinner provided by Mr. King of the Swan Inn. The martial strains of the band were heard to echo in the neighbouring valleys, while bright Sol was a 'smiling spectator' of the pleasing scene.'

'In early April 1858, on a Wednesday at 6 p.m., the school was opened; the company, which included clergy, gentry, farmers, tenants, tradesmen and labourers, sat down to tea after an address by the Rector. The master, Mr. Allen was called upon to address the meeting. In his speech he drew a contrast between the aspect of education now and that of 19 years since when he began his labour as a teacher. The Rector concluded the meeting by saying we are happy to say that the new school opens with upwards of 100 children. An additional room was built on to the school in 1878 for the infants.'

'In March 1879 Mr. Pitt took charge and Mrs. Pitt took the infants and needlework. There were 88-100 scholars.'

'On 1st December, 1924 a new Infants School was built and was dedicated by the Bishop of Chichester. There was a large congregation to witness the ceremony including members of the County Education Authority, the H.M.I., and many neighbouring clergy. The cost of the scheme was about £1,600.'

In 1924, the old school was brought up to standard by the Education Authority by the installation of central heating and the insertion of new windows, etc. In the same year the land to the north of the school building was purchased from Mr. Lee Napper at a cost of £134 and comprised almost an acre to be used as a playground 'or any other pious or charitable purpose'.

In November 1971, this lovely old St. Mary's school and adjoining house were sold by auction by King and Chasemore's for £54,000. Opposite the school were two excellent building plots, each with superb southerly views to the Downs, and these made £8,500 and £8,300 respectively.

Mr. Frank I. Saunders, a Worthing builder, bought the old school building with its two-feet-thick Sussex stone walls, buttresses, high vaulted ceilings and stone-mullioned windows, and the former school-master's house which was part of it. Retaining the original walls to the top-of-door level he built the five present houses keeping the buttresses as features of the new homes and using the old tiles and stone. The boundary wall of the school, also of Sussex stone, was retained for the gardens of the houses.

To the west of the school and behind are seven houses and garages, St. Mary's Close, and on the Common opposite where the infants' school stood are two houses and garages.

When the old school was sold the pupils moved to a new building nearby in Link Lane.

The bells from the three schools are (at the time of writing) housed in the ringing chamber of St. Mary's Church. It would be much nicer if they could be put into glass cases in the new school for everyone to see. I missed the Pulborough one when it ceased to be rung.

The teachers, in 1858, earned as follows: Mr. Allen of Pulborough, £45 per annum and a house; Miss Dallimore of North Heath, £55 per annum with a furnished house with a garden; Miss Odell of Nutbourne, £45 per annum and lodgings.

The only other school in Pulborough is Arundale, which is privately run and is for girls from 5 to 12 years of age, and small boys.

The New Church of England (aided) Primary School

This fine school was first used at Whitsun 1968, when Mrs. Jenkins with one teacher moved with the two top classes. Mr. Winter remained at the old school with the other children until early 1970; he retired later that year.

The official opening took place on 16 January 1972, and the school was dedicated by the Right Rev. Simon Phipps, M.A., Bishop of Horsham.

Mr. Sellick was headmaster from 1 September 1970 until 30 April 1977 when he retired through ill health. Mrs. Jenkins took charge from September 1976 until 31 August 1977. Mr. Ellis became headmaster on 1 September 1977.

There were 293 pupils in May 1980. When this school was opened the oldest living pupil on the register, Mr. S. Marsh, was invited to attend and he sat in the front row with the youngest pupil.

This lovely new school is built in pleasant surroundings. It is a bright modern building with well-equipped classrooms, a spacious hall, modern kitchen and plenty of space for work and play of every description. There is a large games field with equipment for football, cricket, netball, and all sorts of athletics, also a well-equipped library. On 10 June 1972 the Rector, Rev. Basil St. C. Maltin, Chairman of the Managers, officially opened the new swimming pool by unveiling a plaque which said "This Pool was donated by parents and friends of the school". The children eased themselves down the steps into the none-too-warm water and no doubt a lot of children since that day have had the opportunity to learn how to swim. We were not so fortunate in my young days, but it is now a necessity for every child.

The Parent-Teacher Association hold a meeting once a month. They organise a summer fete, Guy Fawkes party, and Christmas Bazaar each year. A Play-Scheme, for the children, is run during the summer holidays by volunteers.

34. Pulborough school and the master's house which was built in 1857-8.

35. Some of the pupils in 1888.

36.   Teachers and pupils in 1904. The author's husband, Clifford, is pictured in the centre of the front row.

37.   After the alterations to the old school. Note the remaining old walls.

38. (*opposite above*) On 1 March 1858 the first stone was laid for a second school in the Pulborough district at North Heath, by the Rev. Sinclair.

39. (*opposite below*) The old school at Nutbourne, which was built in early August 1858, was closed in 1948. It has since been converted to a private house. The original school bell has been replaced.

40. (*above top*) The new Church of England (aided) primary school in Link Lane.

41. (*above*) The swimming pool at the new school on opening day.

Pulborough Village Hall was built in 1931-32. Parishioners worked hard to get this fine hall by buying bricks at 6d. each. Mr. Ern Sheppard did a wonderful job of selling them. Our first carnival in aid of this project was held in 1931. Originally the building was called Pulborough and District Village Hall.

This is an extract from the Carnival and May Revels programme dated Whit Monday 1933:

Pulborough and District Village Hall.

In less than two years and two months, that which the Pessimists said was impossible, has been achieved.

The Pulborough and District Village Hall has been built, furnished, and since the 4th November, 1932, when the building was opened by Her Grace The Duchess of Norfolk, has been used for various purposes on numerous occasions.

The result of the first season has been most encouraging and with the continued support of the local organisations and the district as a whole, there is every reason to believe that the Hall will more than justify its existence year in, year out.

In these pages will be found a statement of the total amount raised and the entire cost of the scheme. These figures show a wonderful result, but our work is not yet complete.

The loan from the West Sussex Rural Community Council has to be discharged, at the latest within five years from the 19th July, 1932. It is, however, gratifying to be able to state that the sum of £57 has already been repaid although that amount is not actually due until July next.

Nevertheless, there is still £228 outstanding and the Committee is anxious to clear off this debt as speedily as possible so that the money may be available for assisting similar schemes elsewhere.

This, then, is the object of the Third Pulborough Carnival.

The net profit from the two previous occasions totalled £557. Surely it should not be an impossible task to raise the sum required by Whit-Monday, 5th June, 1933 ?

There will be numerous attractions, so come in your thousands, bring all your friends, spend as liberally as you can afford and help us to free our Hall from debt.

It must be mentioned that we are again indebted to the Pulborough Women's Institute, who are combining with us once more and whose funds will benefit only to the extent of 30 per cent. of the first £100 profit. Our thanks are due to their Members and to those many other friends who have worked and are still working so hard for the betterment of the social life of the entire district.

In conclusion, I should like to repeat what has already been said on many occasions, that we shall welcome most heartily on the Committee, representatives of those organisations which up to the present have withheld their co-operation.

H. E. DENNIS,

Chairman of the Council of Management.

May, 1933.

Total Amount raised and Cost of Scheme.

Cr.	£	s.	d.		Dr.	£	s.	d.
Donations	577	8	11					
Entertainments, etc. ...	570	7	8	Land	180	0	0
Carnivals, 1931 & 1932	557	6	5	Building as per Contract			
Grant from Carnegie				£1450 0 0			
U.K. Trust	280	0	0	Extras sanc-			
Loan from West Sussex				tioned by			
Rural Community				Committee 133 19 7			
Council ... £285					1583	19	7
Less repaid ... £57				Lighting as per contract	59	16	1
——	228	0	0	Heating ditto ...	185	0	0
Interest on a/c at West-				Furnishing ...	120	3	7
minster Bank ...	39	15	9	Architect's Fee ...	50	0	0
				Legal Charges, etc. ...	26	17	10
				Printing Petty Expenses,			
				etc.	14	16	1
				Total cost of Scheme £2220 13 2			
				Balance at Bank on Capi-			
				tal A c as at 30 4 33 ...	32	5	7
	£2252	18	9		£2252	18	9

On 8 November 1957 the Village Hall Committee held a dance—the 25th anniversary of the opening night—when some 300 people made it a rousing if crowded night. Mr. Bob Baker was M.C. on this occasion. Mrs. S. Rathbone cut a large birthday cake which was decked with 25 lighted candles. The Author was one of the committee members and made a commemorative flower piece for the centre of the stage. Mr. Myram gave a vote of thanks to Mr. Baker at the end of the evening and said he hoped we would all meet again at the Hall's 40th anniversary in 1982. Sad to say, this was not possible as Mr. Baker, Mr. Myram and Mrs. Rathbone were no longer with us.

There have been many functions held in the Village Hall, including Jubilee and Commemoration dances, Victory revels, and numerous other festivities.

In 1968 and 1969, at a cost of £2,500, much work was done, including sanding and sealing the floor, putting in a new floor in the lower hall, providing new stage rear curtains and altering the ladies' cloakroom into a bar. In the near future the committee is hoping to extend the building at the rear.

At the start, the hall was named the Pulborough and District Village Hall, but now the committee has changed it to the Social Centre. It has always been the Village Hall and has this name imprinted over the main entrance.

The only two men left who helped to build it are Mr. Reg Goodsall, who did the central heating and plumbing work, and Mr. Whitewood who did the electrical installations.

The Village Hall is used most days. The Women's Institute have an afternoon and evening group, the Village Produce Association has two flower shows each year, and regular meetings. I wonder how many people know that the V.P.A. started with a market on the pavement before Rivermead bus-stop was made. Whist drives, jumble sales, wedding receptions and birthday parties are held there and the Rother Players and Arundale School use the hall from time to time. The Village Produce Association holds a Carol evening every Christmas, Miss Doris Willmer has only once missed conducting the Carol evening since it started in 1961. An Art and Craft Exhibition is held each year for four days.

42. May Revels in the Oddfellow's field in the early 1920s.

43. The Village Hall was built in 1931-2 by Herbert's, the Pulborough builders, whose premises were on the opposite side of the road.

4. Interior of the Village Hall—the red velvet stage and door curtains, which came from a London theatre, were the gift of Miss Warner.

5. The first carnival procession, 1931, passing along Lower Street.

46. The same carnival, arriving at the Village Hall.

47. The 1934 carnival on its way to the Village Hall field. (*Copyright Garland Collection*)

48. One of the floats in the Whit-Monday carnival procession, 10 June 1935. (*Copyright Garland Collection*)

49. A children's party at the Village Hall, 1937. The author's daughter, Linda, is in the centre of the second row.

50. Victory Revels procession, 10 June 1946, led by the Territorial Band. (*Copyright Garland Collection*)

51. One of the floats representing the Forces Victory Revels. (*Copyright Garland Collection*)

52. One of the main attractions at the Victory Revels—Firewalking Lenz walking bare-
foot on red hot embers. (*Copyright Garland Collection*)

53. Miss Sheila Jennings and her attendants on their way to the Village Hall during the Victory Revels. (*Copyright Garland Collection*)

54. The crowning of the Carnival Queen, 10 June 1946. (*Copyright Garland Collection*)

55. A carnival wending its way along Lower Street.

56. Wilfred and Mabel Pickles in the Village Hall for 'Have a Go', on 22 December 1964. (*Copyright Garland Collection*)

57. The 'Over 60s' Christmas dinner on 6 February 1948, given by the Chanctonbury Lions.

8. The Village Hall committee at the Silver Jubilee dance, 8 November 1957. Left to right—Mr L. Drain, Mrs Greenfield, Mrs Strudwick, Mrs Elliott, Miss . Jennings, Mrs Rathbone cutting the cake, Mr Goodsell, Miss M. Jennings, Mrs Dean and Mr N. Woods.

9. The author with the flower piece which she made to commemorate the Village Hall's Silver Jubilee, 8 November 1957. (*Copyright Garland Collection*)

VIII LIFE AS A SHOP ASSISTANT AT OLIVER'S STORE
EARLY IN THE 1900s

The premises of Oliver's Store in London House, Pulborough, must have been two houses in the first place as there were two stairways, one at each end. One led to the living quarters upstairs which were at ground level at the back due to it being on a hill, and the other stairway led to the drapery stock room and on up to a room under the roof.

This was where my husband Clifford started as an apprentice grocer when he left school in 1913, at the age of 14 years, for a wage of 2s. 6d. per week. In those days it was a shop that sold nearly everything; groceries, drapery, furniture, paraffin oil, methylated spirit, wines and spirits. Shops stayed open then until 7 p.m. on weekdays, 8 p.m. on Fridays and as late as 9 p.m. on Saturdays. Traditionally, Saturday evening was when the wives came in to pay their bills and the husbands followed later, after they had paid their visit to the local. My husband's job was to give each lady a glass of port and each gentleman a glass of beer.

I remember him telling me that one Monday morning, soon after he started to work there, he got a telling-off by Mr. Oliver because Mrs. Knight, from up the road, came in and bought a box of matches; after she had left the shop Mr. Oliver said, 'You knew it was washing day, why didn't you suggest soap, soda, blue, etc., to her, she might have needed them?'. That was his first lesson and one he never forgot. I was also at Oliver's for a few years, in my teens, as book-keeper and cashier, so I learned quite a lot about shop work.

The store for goods such as granulated and demerara sugar, butter, lard, cheese, bacon, currants, sultanas, prunes and dried apricots, etc. was at the top of the garden and all the goods were taken up Potts Lane by horse and cart. The sugar came in two-hundredweight sacks, dried fruit in boxes, and tea in large chests. The paraffin oil was stored in large tanks in a brick-built store at the end of the side passage; this was brought, by the Anglo-American Oil Company, in a large tanker and delivered through a long hose into the tanks and then delivered to the customers in one- and two-gallon cans hanging on the back of the cart.

From the store at the top of the garden the perishable goods had to be carried through the garden and into the shop in all weathers (not so good when the snow was several inches thick). The Cheddar cheeses which weighed 56 lbs. had to be skinned and cut to the customers' needs with a cheese wire, weighed and wrapped; there were also other cheeses such as Edam, etc. Butter and lard were in 28 lb. blocks; the butter had to be cut, weighed, patted and wrapped, the lard was dealt with likewise but not patted. Dried fruits were weighed and wrapped in special blue papers, in a particular way. Sugar was also weighed and packed. Another form of packaging was what was called the 'screws'; these were made with a piece of paper wrapped round the hand, the bottom tucked in and the top turned over and tucked in also. All paper bags had their corners tucked in before being used.

When the customer needed coffee the assistant had to take the beans up two flights of stairs to the room under the roof where the large coffee mill was housed, and there it was ground. Candles were sold in eights and twelves, the eights being longer than the twelves. A machine which was quite a novelty was a small balance scale which was pulled down from the ceiling to weigh the shag, which most men smoked in their pipes. Biscuits were all sold loose and the tins were piled along the front of the counter. The top ones had glass lids but nearly always the customer wanted some out of one of the bottom tins. Bacon came in whole sides which had to be boned and cut into special joints and then all rashers cut by hand. Vinegar came in barrels which had to be put on their sides and tapped. Customers usually brought their own bottles to be filled. The assistant would run off a long list of possible needs to the customer as a reminder— any jam, pickles, sauces, mustard, marmalade, matches, candles, nearly always ending with toilet rolls and emery paper. Tea and many other goods had to be weighed and packed. Nowadays everything is pre-packed and in most shops and supermarkets the assistants only need to fill the shelves. In the early days the ceiling was covered with boots which hung from hooks. These were mostly hob-nailed boots.

The drapery side of the store had its problems as well. The assistant would bring down, from the stock room upstairs, whatever the customer asked for, and more often than not it was not right and another journey up the stairs had to be made. The drapery travellers would come by train and arrive outside the shop by horse and cart with a large hamper which contained their samples; the hamper was left outside and all the samples were brought in by hand. Mrs. Oliver was a good business woman; a customer only had to describe a certain hat or garment and Mrs. Oliver went to London to do the buying. The result was always just what the customer wanted. This was the reason why the property was always called London House; most of the goods came from London. In the first place there were two brothers, Alec and John. John owned the business until 1945 when it was sold to Mr. Tracey.

Two other chores stand out in my memory. The first was connected with a very large blind in a box along the top of the two windows. When the sun came out one of the assistants had to go out with a special long hooked pole, pull the blind down and fix two bars, one each side. Then it would be sure to start to rain or the sun would disappear and up had to go the blind again! The second was the oil lamps in the shop. These were hanging lamps, the mantle type. As any shop is a draughty place when the door opens, the lamps smoked and the mantles turned black and someone had to go round and shake salt on them to clear them.

The assistants, in those days, must have gone home very tired. In 1929 the shops closed at 5.30 p.m. on weekdays, 1 p.m. on Wednesday, 7 p.m. on Fridays, and 8 p.m. on Saturdays. My husband left Oliver's for 10 years, but came back to manage it from 1945 to 1961, at first for Mr. Tracey for five years and later for Mr. Allfrey for 11 years. The drapery department was discontinued in 1945. Mr. Allfrey altered the premises and made the shop much larger. The garden at the back was dug out and the store, which was the old kitchen, was taken into the shop and a new store made where the garden was; most of this was done behind boarded up screens and business continued as usual. The shop was closed for just one week while it was all put in order. We left behind a much larger shop.

Customers' orders were collected from the local and outlying districts by the assistants on bicycles and the orders delivered later in the week by horse and cart. Later, the deliveries were made by motor van.

In this shop there were always four chairs in front of the counters for the customers' use. They liked to have a chat whilst they were being served and the atmosphere was very friendly. It is so different nowadays, especially in the self-service shops; usually the only person you speak to is the girl sitting there waiting to take your money. I often wonder what our great-grandparents would say if they could come back and see how things have altered.

In 1933, J. S. Oliver was advertising men's suits, made to measure, from 38s. 6d. This advertisement appeared in the programme for the Carnival and May Revels on Whit Monday of that year.

During the summer of 1954, while we were at London House, a coach full of Chelsea Pensioners, on their way to the coast, stopped for refreshments at the *Arun Hotel*. They looked very smart in their bright red uniforms.

60. A photograph of the general store in 1922, showing the legend on the wall— Oliver Bros. London House, Draper, Grocer and Furniture dealer. Mr J. S. Oliver and the author's husband stand in the doorway with another assistant, named Cooper, in the centre. Note the overhanging oil lamp.

61. (*right*) Chelsea Pensioners having a break before going on to the coast in 1954. The staff with them are, left to right, Mr Strudwick, Brian Burtenshaw, Joan Marsh and Betty Ruff.

62. (*below*) A view of the shop after it had been enlarged. The back of the old shop ended where the chairs now are, and the new store is at the rear. (*Copyright Garland Collection*)

IX CHANGES IN PULBOROUGH

As you look around Pulborough a lot of the smaller houses were built many years ago and a good many have now been demolished to make way for new buildings. This, they say, is progress—to me it has spoilt the village that I knew for so many years.

Six houses named Malt-house Buildings were demolished where Allfrey Plat now stands. This building consists of 15 flats; 12 single-person and three two-person units, a common room, and resident caretaker-warden flat. There are communal facilities which include a sitting room, laundry room, and kitchenette; also a call bell system for use in emergencies.

Two houses called Ferrymead, which stood next to the Corn Exchange, are now shops. Skeyne House was taken, along with a converted railway carriage (which was the home of the Walker family for years) and a field to the east of Skeyne House, for blocks of flats. Laurel Mount, which was a lovely old house and last owned by Mr. Chandler, is now Laurel Estate consisting of five (what the villagers call upside-down) houses with sleeping quarters downstairs and living quarters upstairs. This enables the occupants to have a good view of the South Downs when they are relaxing.

Tribe's butcher's shop and house (a tin hut used in the past by the Salvation Army) was where Mr. Joe Croucher started his hairdressing business. In 1935 he transferred across the road, opposite the Post Office. When Mr. Croucher moved out, Mr. Duvall (the butcher at Tribe's) used the tin hut as a garage, and later it was taken over by Mr. Smith who used it as a fish shop. Mrs. Smith later lived in the house after losing her husband. Eventually all the property was demolished and is now the Post Office car park.

When Mr. Croucher retired in 1960, Mr. G. Barlow took over the business. He had already worked with Mr. Croucher for ten years.

Booker's workshop and part of the old lane is now a bungalow, Number 147A Lower Street.

Pain's of Arundel, the ironmongers, which was just inside the entrance to the right at the top of Station Hill is now Sotheby, King and Chasemore.

It may interest readers to know that the Corn Exchange, which was part of the old *Swan* Hotel in the 1890s, held a market for corn every Friday, a fair on Easter Tuesdays for toys and pedlery, and a stock market every other Monday. In later years it was used for concerts, dances, whist drives, Boys' Club, etc. I was one of the committee for organising whist drives there all through the last war and we handed over a large sum of money to the Red Cross during this time.

There is quite a selection of hotels and public houses in Pulborough so no one needs to go thirsty! The *Arun* in Lower Street is said to have been gutted by fire many years ago in the time of the horse-drawn fire engine. One of the horses dropped dead after making the journey from Petworth.

Miss Gander and Miss Storey were the first to own *Chequers*, at the top of Church Hill. It was then in the house opposite the church steps. Mr. Stourmont added 'Campbells' shop, altered it and made both into one large hotel. This was originally a 16th-century property. It used to be the *Chequers* Inn and Posting House where a change of horses was made on the London to Chichester Road. I was given to understand that two spare horses were always kept at the *Swan* Hotel; they were used with the others to pull the coaches up Church Hill. They were then changed and the two original horses were taken back to rest ready for the next coach. Before this time *Chequers* Inn seems to have been connected with a monastery dating back at least to the time of Henry IV and a little picturesque chapel, which stood apart from the main building at the rear, was used as a delightful recreation room for games; table tennis, darts and other indoor games.

The annexe across the road also belonged to the *Chequers*. In the early hours of Friday 15 November 1963, the main hotel was destroyed by fire; damage was estimated at £30,000. The noise from the burning timbers of the old building was heard for a considerable distance. Seven elderly women guests, the sole occupants, were rescued from their beds unhurt. The cobbler's shop of Mr. A. Campbell, which was built into the hotel on the London Road, was also damaged by smoke and water. Firemen from Billingshurst, Petworth and Storrington took nearly five hours to get the fire under control. Police Sergeant P. Penfold helped to rescue the occupants who spent the rest of the night in the annexe across the road. The proprietress, Mrs. Elizabeth Searancke, took over the hotel (her first) in 1960. The little chapel at the rear escaped the fire. This hotel was never rebuilt; the original annexe is now used as the *Chequers* Hotel.

The present public houses are; the *Red Lion*, Lower Street, the *Five Bells*, London Road, the *Rose and Crown*, Codmore Hill, the *White Horse*, Marehill, the *White Hart*, Stopham and *The Oddfellows* in Lower Street, next to the village Hall. This last, I think, must be the oldest; the buildings are thought to be around 500 years old. Until 1968 the pub only sold beer and cider but since then it has been fully licensed. The earliest documentary evidence of *The Oddfellows* is a copy of an insurance policy issued by the Sun Insurance Company, dated 23 August 1757, insuring it as a farm with two barns and livestock.

At the east end of Pulborough there are some lovely old cottages. 'Sales' had a thatched roof and it was called Bedstead Corner as there were a lot of iron bed-ends around the garden. 'Sales' was burnt down in 1909 when a spark from a passing traction engine set light to the thatch. It was rebuilt in 1912.

At the top of the lane to the left of 'Sales' there are some very old properties. What was No. 1 Rock Cottages has been renamed 'Old Farm Cottage'. This was, originally, two cottages with ladders to the bedrooms; the Victorian part was added 100 years ago.

No. 2 Rock Cottages was also two cottages years ago. There is a large open fireplace with the bread oven at the side. The chimney goes right up through the middle and upstairs it was possible to walk all the way round it. The late owner may have altered the house.

The cottage after you pass 'Sales' is 'Le-Bijou'; in my young days this was two cottages which housed two large families, the Floats and the Wellsteds.

The next cottage is quite small but, like the others, must be very old. Mrs. Johnstone, of Bignor Park, had Holme Manor built and it was finished in 1914. She was a previous owner of 'Sales'.

The last house just before the entrance to Holme Manor was built as stables for Holme Manor and converted during the last war.

In Mare Hill there are numerous old cottages—I think 'King's' is the oldest. There are 51 cottages which make up this very picturesque part of Pulborough, most of which have remained the same through the ages. There are a few modern ones. In the past there was a cobbler's shop, a public house, and a sub-Post Office here. Before the road was made there was only one way. This started off from the right a little way along Broomers Hill road, went across the Common, through a twitten between 'Twitten House' and 'Le-Swin' to what was then the public house (now 'Sunnyside'), through another twitten between 'Sunnyside' and 'Marestone's' and so to the main road. These twittens can still be seen.

Two very attractive cottages are 'Pear Trees' and 'Yeomans'; the owners (the sixth) are Mr. and Mrs. T. Walker.

'Pear Trees' was built sometime in the 18th century, as the dwelling house and what is now 'Yeomans' was the barn belonging to it. The earliest records show that it then belonged to the Leconfield Estate. The barn was converted into a 'two-up, two-down' cottage and sold to a private owner in 1899. There were many agricultural tenants in the early days. In 1952 the first alterations were made. The cottages are now separated and an extra wing has been added on the right of 'Yeomans'. From the bedroom there is a veranda which has a wonderful view stretching from Chanctonbury to Goodwood.

The shop joining the *White Horse* was for many years a grocer's and general provision merchant, pork butcher and drapers.

63. The last of the six cottages to be demolished on the site where Allfrey Plat now stands.

64. Allfrey Plat, which consists of 15 flats—12 single-person and three two-person units—supervised by a resident warden. Communal facilities include a sitting-room, laundry and kitchenette, and a call-bell system for use in emergencies.

65. Three of the five old cottages in Lower Street, which were demolished to make way for a block of flats and the veterinary surgeon's premises.

66. This block of flats named Heron Rye replaced the old cottages.

67. Cecil Strudwick's cycle shop with his house at the rear. It was demolished to make way for the Arun Service Station.

68. Killick's house, shop and bakehouses on the right. This is now the site of three maisonettes called Riverview, and the doctors' surgery, which transferred from Church House on 4 March 1978.

69. The doctors' new surgeries.

70. Tribe's butcher's shop and adjoining house. Both were demolished to make way for the Post Office car park.

71. Miss Gardener's cottage on the left, now a shop called 'Salindra'.

71a. Detail of Plate 71.

72. The *Swan Hotel* and Corn Exchange, demolished in 1958, stood where the new *Swan Hotel* and shops now stand. This photograph, *c.* 1900, shows Mr and Mrs Jennings, the proprietors, and relations, in their carriage-and-four ready to set off for Goodwood races. With them on the back seat is Charlie Craven. Standing beside the carriage are Mr Smith and Mr Sturgess, and Mat Wadey holding the horses.

72a. Detail of Plate 72.

73.   The *Arun Hotel* in 1884. Note the stables on the left.

74.   The *Water's Edge*, near the railway station, which in the past was the *Railway Hotel* and Assembly Rooms. Not very attractive since the front entrance and windows were filled in.

75. The *Chequers Hotel* before it was destroyed by fire.

76. The *Chequers Hotel* after the fire of 15 November 1963.

77. This 15th-century chapel, which stood at the rear of the *Chequers Hotel*, was saved from the fire. (*Photo by kind permission of Ashley Courtenay*)

78. The *Red Lion*.

79. The *Five Bells* in London Road. Hampshire's butcher's shop can be seen on the right. Note the bad state of the road

80. The ruins of the *Rose and Crown*, Codmore Hill, after the fire of 1915.

81. The *White Horse*, Mare Hill, with the shop and the old Congregational chapel.

82. The *White Hart*, Stopham, one mile west of Pulborough. Damaged by floods on 15 September 1968.

83. The *Oddfellows*, Lower Street, with Mr Short's little butcher's shop on the right.

83a. Sales Cottage, 1908, before the fire.

84. The first cottage on the left is 'Le-Bijou'.

85. 'Yeomans' at Mare Hill, converted from an old barn.

X POSTAL HISTORY OF PULBOROUGH

Kelly's Directory of 1899 had this entry.

Post, M. O. & T. O., **T.** M. O., Express Delivery, Parcel Post, S. B. & Annuity & Insurance Office (Railway Sub-Office. Letters should have R.S.O. Sussex).— Clement Ansell, postmaster. Letters arrive from London & all parts at 1.27 & 10.20 a.m. & 5.30 p.m.; dispatched at 11.45 a.m. 12.30, 5.15 & 7.45 p.m.; sunday delivery, 6.45 a.m.; dispatch, 5.30 p.m. Money orders are granted & paid from 8 a.m. to 8 p.m. Telegraph office open, week days, from 8 a.m. to 8 p.m.; sunday, 8 to 10 a.m. There is a telegraph office at the railway station

This must have applied to the Post Office when it was situated at the top of Church Hill. In the Boer War period Clement Ansell was Postmaster. He was succeeded by William Henry Parsons Wooley whose salary was £118 per annum and he in turn was succeeded by Frederick Waller in July 1909.

The building in Lower Street was first used as a Post Office in December 1906. The property was leased to the Post Office by a Mr. Albert Edward Comper until May 1952, when it was purchased as Crown property by the then Postmaster General for the sum of £4,000. Until July 1953 the Post Office was controlled by the Head Postmaster, Petworth, since when the control has been under the Head Postmaster, Worthing.

Horse-drawn mail vans were used up to the outbreak of World War I and postmen delivered mail to the outlying districts on bicycles, morning and afternoon. One of the horse-drawn mail vans left Petworth each evening at 7 o'clock calling at Fittleworth Sub-Post Office on the way. The driver handed over the Petworth mail at the Post Office, collected the London mail from the station, took it back to the office and after sorting it made the return journey to Petworth, calling at Fittleworth Sub-Post Office and arriving at Petworth in the early hours of the morning.

For many years a similar journey was made each day by my father-in-law, F. W. Strudwick, in the opposite direction, leaving Pulborough Post Office early in the morning, calling at Storrington Post Office in Church Street and then on to Washington and Ashington delivering mail. He stayed at Ashington until late afternoon bringing back the mail from Ashington, Washington and Storrington to Pulborough in the evening. The mail van was provided by the Post Office but he had to provide his own ponies. He always kept two so that one could be rested every other day. Mr. Strudwick gave his ponies a pinch of saltpetre every morning and had a pinch himself for, as he said, what was good for the ponies was good for himself. He certainly was a very nimble man and was never once late on duty. He was living at 'Sunnyside', which was opposite the

Post Office (after it opened in Lower Street) and he would go round knocking up the other postmen who lived in the street before he went on duty.

In 1968 second class mail was introduced and in 1976 the Post Office gave up collecting mail on Sundays.

In 1980 the general public were very worried as there were rumours that the Post Office was going to be closed altogether. This was denied by the Postmaster. Strange things had been happening to the floor in the public part and there was concern about the structure.

To speed up deliveries of letters for local addresses, Pulborough Post Office has arranged for these to be posted, marked 'local', in a specially-marked box. This means that they will not be sent to Redhill for sorting. Letters can also be handed to the postman on his rounds.

At first, when the postal system as we know it started in the 1840s, letters were taken to the main centres to be delivered by the Post Office, but by 1852 letter boxes had been erected in certain places. There are still two of the original type in use, both in the Channel Islands. Extension of the scheme to the mainland was in 1853 and one dated 1853 still survives in Dorset. The four oldest in the Pulborough district are as illustrated.

86. Pulborough Post Office was situated at the top of Church Hill until December 1906; the premises were then taken over by a shoe repair shop.

Post Office, Pulborough

87. (*right*) This 1907 photograph shows the oil lamp hanging outside the Post Office.

88. (*below*) Mr W. F. Strudwick driving through Storrington in the Royal Mail van in 1911.

89. Mr Strudwick stabled his ponies in the barn on the right of the picture which then belonged to 'Henleys'. It is now the site of the bus stop.

90. Postal uniforms through the ages, as portrayed by Worthing men in the 1980 August Bank Holiday Carnival at Worthing.

91. The oldest letter box in the Pulborough district at Little Bognor. It is a wall box (no. 2) (small), cast by Smith & Hawkes, 1861-71.

92. This letter box is at Bignor, wall box type C (small) cast by Smith & Hawkes, 1871-1881.

93. A letter box at Wiggonholt, wall box type B (medium) cast by W. T. Allen & Co. during the period 1881-1904.

94. This letter box is on the wall of the down platform at Pulborough station, dating from 1900. It is a wooden bracket box as provided by the Office of Works for use on ships, at railway stations and large government offices.

XI THE BUS SERVICE

The local bus service originates from 1904 when a company named the Sussex Motor Road Car Company Limited was first formed. The Company introduced the first No. 1 service between Pulborough station and Worthing using steam buses. A special well was dug in a field opposite the *Frankland Arms* at Washington as they had to be rather particular about the water for the boilers. The fares from Pulborough were as follows—to Mare Hill 2d., Wiggonholt Common 3d., Cootham 6d., Storrington 9d., Washington 1s.0d., Findon, 1s. 6d., Worthing 1s. 9d. In the middle of 1906, however, the service had to be withdrawn as the Road Car Company found itself in debt.

The Worthing Motor Services was formed in 1909 and a service between Worthing and Storrington was one of those operated by this concern, but it was not until 29 September 1946 that the Southdown extended the service to Pulborough. At this time, the service ran every day on an hourly timetable, the journey taking one hour and four minutes direct or one hour and fourteen minutes on journeys routed via West Chiltington Village. I'm sorry to say we have now lost our hourly No. 1 service.

The Sunday extension of the Worthing to Storrington service to Petworth was made in 1925 but this was withdrawn in 1928.

The service No. 22 ran for many years between Brighton and Petworth—it actually commenced operation in 1921 and was extended to Midhurst in 1951. This service was later re-numbered 59/61 and extended to Petersfield. Nowadays the service has been drastically cut.

During the early years milk churns were picked up along the route. It was normal on certain buses for the gangways to be filled with the churns.

The service offered by mini-bus is a great help to people living at Codmore Hill and Stane Street as it enables the residents to come into the village to do their shopping and collect their pension.

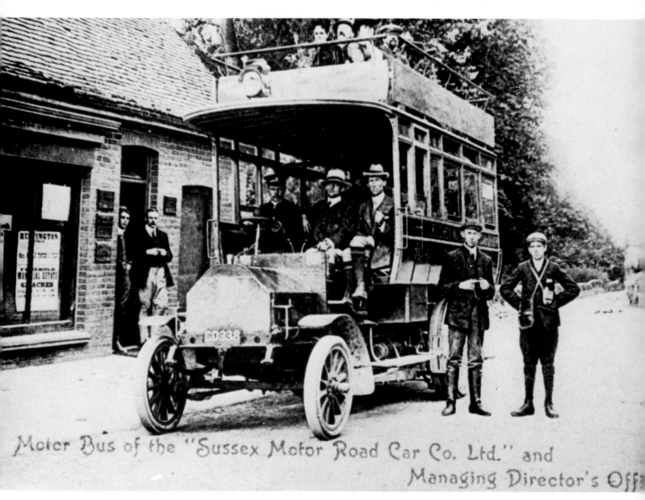

Motor Bus of the "Sussex Motor Road Car Co. Ltd." and
Managing Director's Off[...]

95. Mr Newland Tompkins, Managing Director of the first No. 1 Bus Company sitting in the centre with Mr St Aubyn on his left. This photograph was taken outside Mr Newland Tompkins' Auctioneers' office in Station Road (now Hamilton Cole Sussex Ltd.) in 1904.

96. (*opposite above*) The No. 1 bus filling up with passengers.

97. (*opposite below*) One of the new Southdown vehicles, shortly after delivery in 1948.

XII WOMEN'S INSTITUTE

May I tell you a little about the Women's Institute which I joined on 22 August 1937?

The first W.I. was started in Canada in 1897 and began in a very simple way, the members meeting in each other's houses to exchange ideas. Mrs. Alfred Watt, M.A., M.B.E., watched the birth and growth of the Women's Institute movement in Canada. With a band of courageous women on 11 September 1915, and with the blessing and support of the Board of Agriculture, started the first Women's Institute in the British Isles at a meeting in a small creeper-smothered garden room at Llanfairpwll in Anglesey.

In West Sussex the first W.I. was formed in Singleton and East Dean in 1915. This movement has grown until it has become one of the largest organisations for women in the world.

All W.I. members have a share in governing their Institute; they decide what the Institute will do and how it will spend its funds and every year they elect a committee to carry out the Institute's decisions and to do the routine business.

Each County has a County Committee; ours is West Sussex County Federation Executive Committee, elected each year by the West Sussex Institutes. The affairs of the movement are settled by the Institutes themselves through the Council meetings held twice a year in the County and through the Annual General Meeting of the National Federation to which each W.I. is entitled to send a delegate.

The Women's Institutes in the same district are arranged into Groups which meet twice a year in conference. Our group is the Pulborough Group, formed in September 1918.

The Institute is a common meeting ground for women of all classes, denominations and political parties; we therefore avoid discussion on sectarian and party matters but we try to work together for the benefit of our homes and country life as a whole.

At our monthly meetings, which take place in the Village Hall, we discuss and decide questions of Institute business, we learn together about the things which interest us, and we join in games and entertainments. We still have a very good drama group. We go to meetings not just to look on but to share our knowledge and experience and we show the true Institute spirit when we help towards the success of our meetings with that friendliness and goodwill which is the essential part of W.I. life.

Our meetings begin with the singing of 'Jerusalem', followed by business matters. Each month we have either a competition or exhibition, as well as a speaker or demonstration. We run a raffle, and sales-table where members can bring goods to sell giving a percentage to our Institute. We finish the meeting with a cup of tea and a chat. There are two sick visitors. Several years ago we 'adopted' two men at St. Bridget's Home, East Preston. Two of our members visit them each month, and sometimes take them out to tea. We send gifts on their birthdays and Christmas.

During the summer outings and rambles are organised. For many years we have entered, and sometimes won, the competition at Ardingly. There is also an evening Institute—'Pulborough Meadows', which was formed in 1956 for the benefit of those unable to attend in the afternoon.

88. The Drama Group in the village play of 1956. Left to right are: Mrs Goodsell; Miss Ellis; Mrs Willmer; Mrs Knight; Mrs Brown; Mrs Boxall; Mrs Chandler; Miss Newbery; Mrs Pavey; Mrs Medlock; Mrs Burt and Mrs Puttock. (*Copyright Garland Collection*)

89. 1973 was 'Plant a Tree Year'. Miss Malcolm, the then President, planted a redhawthorn at the primary school, watched by Mrs Cousins, Mrs Young, Mrs Hope-Gill, Miss Morell, Mrs Jones, Mrs Thompson, Miss Moore, Mrs Glazier, Mr Sellick and a large number of school children.

100. W.I. members preparing sandwiches for the teas at the carnival in 1970.

101. Denman College, planned, paid for and furnished by members of the W.I. was opened by Sir Richard Livingstone in 1948. Members can attend for five-day or week-end courses. This college is the W.I.'s most valuable asset.

102.   A photograph taken at the rear of the doctors' surgery and Riverview flats after a lunch to celebrate the Diamond Jubilee on 21 September 1978.

103.   An outing to Wilton House in 1972 when husbands were invited to accompany their wives. Shown are Mrs Cullen, Mrs Greatorex, Miss Vallens, Mrs Cole, Mrs Phillipson, Miss Watkins, Mr & Mrs Fowler, Mr & Mrs Madell, Miss Jones, Mr & Mrs Jackson, Mrs R. Goodsell, Mrs Knight, Mr & Mrs Stone, Mrs Clare, Mr & Mrs Corden, Mrs Bolitho, Miss Malcolm, Mrs Hatfield, Miss Morell, Miss Fagence, Mrs Hennings, Mrs Withers and Mrs Wright.

XIII HISTORIC HOUSES AND BRIDGES

Several 18th- and 19th-century houses face St. Mary's church; further down the road you will come to Old Place which was erected in the reign of Henry VI and was formerly one of the seats of the Apsley family. The stone masons who built the nave, aisles and tower of St. Mary's church are thought to have been employed in building this splendid house. One of the barns, thought to have been part of the original Manor, has been converted into a house and still has much of the 15th- and 16th-century flavour about it. There is also quite a large pond at the side, where many people years ago used to skate.

The Old Mill, nearby, was in working order until 1927 and it was interesting for us children to watch the big wheel turning and the water splashing as it went around. The mill was empty for several years but eventually, in 1936, it was bought and converted into a very attractive private residence with the mill stream running under the centre. The old mill stones were laid in the garden and can still be seen. The stream starts at the other side of New Place pond; it used to run into the Rectory pond, then under the London Road (this has all been drained underground since the Rectory pond was filled in and Harwood's garage built over the top), then it wends its way into Old Place pond, on to Coombelands pond and finishes in the river Arun. The little cottage called the 'Nag' near Old Mill at Old Place was used as a cart shed in my young days.

The Manor of Pulborough is first mentioned in Domesday Book. The original Manor was most likely on the site of the 'Motte' or moat, now preserved near the Ambulance Station.

New Place Manor as we know it today was built in 1252 A.D.; it is situated on high ground overlooking many miles of the South Downs. The house itself was built by order of King Henry III after the original house was burnt down. The Windsor Records state that 'the order was given to Alard-Le-Flemming and his heirs as his houses in his Manor of Puleburg were lately burned by accident that it may be rebuild in this part of Pulberge where his ancestors used to inhabit, as he thinks best, without crenellating'. It descended in his family until about 1450 when it passed to the Apsley family, after which it descended to the Shelley family (cousins of the poet who lived in Horsham).

What remains of the house now is only part of the original building; the house at one time was at least twice its present size. It did have an underground passage, and an 80-ft. well cut through the solid rock in 1252. It has still got its wall 'Pleasance'. The spiral staircase has been destroyed but remains of the door can be seen in the south wall of the Great Hall.

When I was a girl Mr. and Mrs. Brockhurst lived there; in those days it was a farm and most of the fields around belonged to them and were cultivated. We lived in London Road and each day, with our own milk can, we would go and fetch the milk. Since then it has had several owners; Max Factor used it during the war. It has also been a Guest House and a Country Club, and at present is owned by Mr. and Mrs. Crossley. During the first World War the pond was drained and all the fish were sent to help feed people in the towns.

Coombelands, standing in a large garden, was once a farm and employed a full outside staff to work in the gardens and on the farm, as well as a number of indoor staff from a scullery maid to lady's maid and a butler. There were underground passages once used for smuggling. In a very old newspaper cutting it states

'Ghost with eyes of fire. Something between a fox and an elephant. The nerves of the inhabitants of the little Sussex town of Pulborough are in a very staccato condition at the present moment. There was something immense and indefinable wandering loose in the dark roads and fields on the verge of which the District Council's oil lamps cease to make the darkness of the night visible. What Stephen Hunt, from Worthing, saw at 7.20 p.m. on the night of Friday 17th (year not known, circa 1900) before he rushed into the snug little bar parlour of Ye Olde Fyve Bells Inn, a complete nervous wreck, shaking from head to foot with the blood gone from his cheeks and with a nameless fear in his protruding eyes, is not known. He was a plain Sussex man, sober and hard working. He is the very last type of man to be affected by a ghost story. He had, every night for months, returned alone on the mile of road between Coombelands and Pulborough and nothing had happened but this very night he was passing down the familiar drive and had just reached the bridge that crosses the pond when out of the shadows of the trees an enormous shape loomed up. In his first description it was as big as an elephant but after a while it came down to larger than a fox. He was positive it had two great fiery eyes that shone in the darkness and with a diabolical groan it brushed past him. Thinking it was a practical joker he was angry at being startled; he gave chase but before he had passed the pond it had vanished. Then the dread of the supernatural settled down on his soul, his blood froze in his veins, his heart almost stopped its beating; never a more scared man stood terror-stricken on a lonely countryside. He took to his heels and got himself with as much speed as might be to Pulborough.'

For some months he had been employed as a carpenter in the rebuilding of Coombelands which had been purchased from the Rt. Hon. Sir Henry Fletcher, M.P. by Mr. Burnett.

The story of the ghost and the story of the house are clearly bound up with one another. Nearly fourteen months after the rebuilding started some mysterious things were discovered. In the first place, extraordinary secret passages and caves were found beneath the old house; also forbidding tunnels reeking with suggestions of crimes committed in the old days when unwelcome guests were done to death and their bodies disposed of in the brief space between midnight and a summer dawn. Moreover, in pulling down the oak wainscotting from above a fireplace a mass of human bones was discovered. Sometime afterwards, when the new house was practically completed, a caretaker was placed in the establishment in the shape of Mr. Burnett's housekeeper. Like Stephen Hunt, this lady was not superstitious, but Coombelands was too much for her. Weird noises haunted her in the daytime and something like human groans disturbed her rest at night. She could not get to sleep—the place was clearly haunted. Quite a large part of the original farm is now owned by Mr. Guy Harwood the well-known racehorse trainer.

Hardham Priory, now converted to a farmhouse, was once a small establishment of the Austin Canons and was dissolved, like so many monastic houses, in the 16th century. The Priory has, for long, been the home of the Ash family, well-known Sussex farmers.

Stopham House was known in earlier times as La Forde or Ford Place and is said to have been the residence of the ancient family of Ford or Forde, so called from the ford of the River Arun. This ford was replaced first by a ferry known as Estover Ferry and afterwards by the present seven-arched bridge which is still one of the best, as well as the most picturesque, structures of its kind in the county. For a number of years, Stopham House was a home for the elderly but a little while ago it was converted into private flats.

Cordens, the chemist's shop, is a 17th-century building. It has been a chemist's since

1860 and since 1887 the Cordens have kept it in the family for four generations. Mr. Louis Corden was the first of the line and among his descendants were eight pharmacists. Two of them, Mr. Victor Corden and his son Dennis, are now in charge of the Pulborough firm. In their shop they still have the nest of drawers from which the first Mr. Corden sold bees-wax, juniper-gum, cascara-bark, gentian-root, linseed and all of the other homely remedies and household concoctions of the Victorian age. Now you can buy cosmetics, and toiletries as well as modern medicines. In these days of declining service it is a remarkable survival from the past that the Cordens keep their shop open until 7 p.m. Mondays, Tuesdays, Thursdays and Fridays, 1 p.m. on Wednesdays and 6.30 p.m. on Saturdays. They are a very kind and helpful family and their shop is a pleasure to go into.

Before it became a chemist's shop the building was a public house called *The Running Horse.* In the days of the coach and horses the coachmen would stay here and their masters and families at the old *Swan* Hotel opposite. It was a sad day in 1958 when this lovely old hotel and the Corn Exchange were demolished to make way for a modern hotel. There was a shop and house right in the middle of the road, just around the corner on the Arundel road between Cordens and the *Swan* Hotel, owned by Harry Fielder. This was a fish shop and greengrocer's. Harry went to Worthing most days in his two-wheeled fish float to get a supply of fresh fish. Snowey, Harry's brother, owned 'Small Beer Dyke Pig Farm' and knackers yard on the Nutbourne Road.

Lloyds Bank is a very old building. This was a private house until Lloyds took possession several years ago. It was once owned by Miss Wickens who ran a small private school, gave piano lessons, and played the organ at Wiggonholt church.

In the centre of the village is a 15th-century cottage renamed Pulborough House. While the building was being renovated for the present owner the decorators, after taking off the old wall-paper, discovered a painting of a man's face. Experts think it may date back to the time of Oliver Cromwell, more than 300 years ago. There is evidence of more paintings in the same room, possibly of a leaf design.

Wharfe House was once the home of Benny Butler, who was a carpenter, until 1930. It was taken over by Mr. W. J. Allfrey and extra living accommodation added. In late 1930 more living accommodation was added and yet another addition—the offices—in 1946. Wharfe House (the name speaks for itself) had a road at the side leading to the river. No doubt it was used for loading and unloading barges.

Part of Henley's in Lower Street dates back to the 1600s. It is thought to have been rebuilt by Mr. Henley in 1708 on the original cellars. Window tax was imposed in 1695, so it would appear that the windows shown blank were built that way to be opened up later if required. Before 1851, when the window tax was removed, the two end east rooms were added with an attic above. The grounds extended and joined to No. 125 Lower Street, with a public footpath running through from Lower Street to the meadows in the south before Rivermead was developed. The kitchens were in the basement. A pump in the cellar was pumped manually to get the water into the tank in the attic. This property was owned by Thomas Lucas who, in the 1870s, ran a small coaching establishment for boys. They slept in the attic rooms which had only a small window at the east and west ends. Mr. Lucas died on the 19 May 1878. The house was left to his daughter, Jane, who was married to the Rev. Frederick Jarrett then living at Goodleigh, Devon.

In 1911 the Rev. F. Jarrett came back to live with his second wife and daughter, Margaret. After his death in 1934 it was sold to G. R. Newberry. From 1934 to 1952 it was part of the 'Spring Green Lady' guest house. Captain William Forsayeth owned it from 1952 to 1953. In 1953 the present owners, Mr. and Mrs. W. R. Hutcheson, bought it and occupied it as a family house and later used it for a small architectural practice.

From the W.I.'s 'A Pulborough Scrap Book' (1947) comes this entry: 'Pulborough Poor House. In the year 1811 a "Vestry Meeting" (Pulborough) came to this agreement— "That Mr. Lucas (owner of the land on which St. Margaret's was yet to be built) shall build a wall between his garden (that of the future St. Margaret's) and the Poor House garden belonging to the Parish of Pulborough, the wall to extend from the Poor House in a straight line to square with the other end. It must be of "not less than ten feet in height" (the Parish will help pay the cost) and if the Parish thinks proper they will plant trees and nail against the wall (a plan showed the Poor House to adjoin Mr. Lucas's land on the east, its garden appears to have been of great length).' The Document ends: 'The above is a true copy'; it was signed by James Heath and Kidman, Churchwardens and John Cooter and _____, Overseers'.

To return to the re-discovered Poor House (now occupied by Arundale School), Mrs. A. E. Knight, née Burbury, says that her own house and the row of cottages extending westwards to St. Margaret's were all part of the institution's buildings. Its garden was large. How long the Poor House was in use seems unknown.

Lane End was the first house to be built, for Mr. Benger, in 1922 or 1923 in what was then just a field. Since then seven more houses have been built. They all have a wonderful view extending to the South Downs.

Hardham Mill and House were formerly owned by Mr. Eames and managed by Mr. Duke; they were situated on the River Rother which joins the River Arun just below Stopham Bridge. The mill was demolished before the house and the timbers were used in building the Mill Lane houses at the east end of Pulborough.

Sited adjacent to the River Rother are the Hardham works of the West Sussex Southern Water Authority. An order sanctioned by the Ministry in 1950 provided for the construction of an intake and weir across the River Rother. The first stage of the existing water treatment was commissioned by the North West Sussex Board in 1954 as a direct river abstraction works. The West Sussex Water Authority is the successor to the North West Sussex Board and the water supply area of the Division has existed in its present form since 1961.

The statutory area of supply covers 374 square miles and extends from the South Downs north to the Surrey border and from the Hampshire border east to the London/ Brighton road. The Division caters for an estimated population of 200,000 and includes industry and the towns of Crawley and Horsham. The two main sources of supply for the Division are Weir Wood near East Grinstead and the River Rother at Hardham.

In recent years a number of boreholes have been developed within the Hardham area, both to supplement the river source and to provide back-up standby facilities when the river source is limited either for reasons of quantity or quality. Five boreholes are currently capable of operating and others are due for remedial work or commissioning in the course of the next year. In the 1970s the Authority recognised the urgent need for additional water treatment plant at Hardham to meet the needs of the fast growing areas of Crawley and Horsham and industry in West Sussex.

By the year 2001 it is anticipated that demand on the Hardham source from these areas will increase by at least 40 per cent. At the time of writing there is an enormous amount of work taking place on further enlargement. Huge cranes can be seen from the main road. Prior to this the firm of Duke & Ockenden made the first borehole for the Chanctonbury Rural District Council at Nutbourne pumping station in 1930/31.

According to an account in the *West Sussex Gazette* of 31 May 1973, the building once known as the Iron Castle was a twenty-six-roomed edifice of Sussex sandstone. The stone was quarried from his own land by Dr. John Harley in about 1903. Dr. Harley is believed to have helped to build the pseudo-castle, which has four turrets, some reached by spiral staircases, an entrance hall 43 ft. long and 26 ft. wide, round which runs the balcony, two staircases and a billiards room.

The house, now known as The Beedings, stands 300 ft. above sea level, at the end of a quarter-mile long drive. From its 60 ft. high flat roof there are some magnificent views over three counties. It is understood that Dr. Harley designed the Castle himself, using steel beams and reinforced concrete on the inside, creating walls 14 ins. thick in places. All the floors are made of terrazzo and some of the principal rooms are very large. Dr. Harley lived in the Castle, which was sometimes known as Harley's Castle, until his death in 1921 at the age of eighty and then his daughter Miss Phyllis Harley lived there until 1930. The house was occupied for a time, then taken over by the military during the war. In the grounds there is a coach-house with room for four coaches and accommodation. I was informed that Dr. Harley was terrified of fire as his wife had died in a fire in an ordinary house.

The Toat Monument occupies a hilltop to the north-west of Pulborough. It was erected in 1823 in memory of Samual Drinkald, a London tea merchant, by his two sons, one of whom lived at Lowfold, and was a well-known cock-fighter and racehorse owner in his time. He owned Toat and Amblehurst, the latter a small manor with a barn in which he kept his fighting-cocks. His racehorses were stabled at Shipbourne.

The inscription on the tower reads: 'In memory of Samual Drinkald 1823'.

There were two lovely old stone bridges across the Arun until the 1930s. Clements Bridge, which had three arches, was built in 1799 and was at the end of the Station Road houses. It was originally built to give access to the meadows on the south side of the river. The piers became unsafe and it was taken down. It is sad to see these historic landmarks go.

In the field on the other side of the river there is a large mound made of concrete on which the farmer built his hay-ricks to protect them from floods.

An unusual situation was caused when a new stone bridge, the Swan Bridge, was built alongside the old stone bridge in 1936. Fortunately, the old bridge with its four semi-circular arches was left standing. It was built in 1738 to replace a wooden bridge which was a little farther down stream. In an inquisition held in 1350 a ferry was mentioned in Pulborough.

104. Old Place dates from the 15th century and is built of stone. It retains the original moulded doorways, some fine old oak beams and a gallery in the dining-room.

105. Lovely Mill Cottage, which was converted from the old mill in 1936, is now a very attractive private residence.

106. New Place Manor as we know it today.

107. The famous gateway at New Place Manor which Queen Elizabeth I passed through when she visited the Apsley family in 1591, on her way from Sutton Place, Surrey to Cowdray. To commemorate this visit the renaissance top was added to the existing 14th-century stone work.

108. (*above*) This dovecote at New Place Manor is believed to be the only existing 16th-century one in Europe. It was reconstructed in the 19th century retaining the earlier mullioned windows.

109. (*right*) This very unusual chimney is at the west end of New Place Manor.

110. (*top*) Coombelands is a Queen Anne property overlooking the River Arun. It was built in 1705 on earlier foundations and over the still existing Tudor cellars.

111. (*above*) Hardham Priory. A disastrous fire occurred in 1912 which gutted some of the ancient buildings, but much remains that is both picturesque and of antiquarian interest.

112. (*right*) Stopham House. The date of the house is not known, although the hall and adjoining rooms belong to the Tudor era. Much of the old house was pulled down in 1787 and the structure then erected has since been twice remodelled, once in 1842 and again in 1865. In these numerous changes most of the original characteristics of the mansion have been lost.

113. Stopham Bridge, built in 1309 during the reign of Edward II.

114. (*left*) Jubilee Bridge, between the main gates of Stopham House and the gate by the lodge. This very pretty wooden bridge was built by the Bartelott family to commemorate the Diamond Jubilee of Queen Victoria, and to enable them to walk to their land on the other side of the road. It was taken down in 1921 when the Southdown bus service between Brighton and Petworth began.

Jubilee Bridge, Stopham, Pulborough

115. (*top*) Puttock's farm, which is now Stane Street restaurant. There was originally a pond between the farm and the road which has since been filled in.

116. (*above*) The 16th century Old Cottage at the top of Church Hill has cellars which are reported to have been used by smugglers.

116a. Detail of 116.

117. Old Timbers and Horncroft. These lovely timber-framed, 400-year-old cottages at Albury Corner, at the bottom of Church Hill, have a wealth of old timbers, mellow tiles and pretty windows. There is also an old Tudor chimney at the south end of the building.

118. (right) Corden's chemist's shop and house is a 17th century building which has been a chemist's since 1860. The Cordens have kept it in the family for four generations since 1887. Prior to that it was owned by Maddocks, who made and bottled lavender water.

119. Detail of Plate 118.

120. (*above*) The shop on the right was the Corn Stores, owned by E. W. Joyes until 1918.

121. (*left*) H. Fielder's shop, which was demolished in 1935, because it had become a danger spot with the increase in traffic.

122. (*below*) Demolition of H. Fielder's shop in 1935.

123.   Lloyds Bank, with the finest *Magnolia Grandiflora* you will see around here on the right.

124.   Pulborough House was once part of the property owned by Killick's the bakers. This could have been their first shop—the date is not known.

125. Wharfe House on the right, as it was before the extra accommodation and offices were added in 1930.

126. Tudor Park Farm, which is off the Stopham Road about halfway between the railway station and Stopham Bridge.

127. Henleys, Lower Street, is in the statutory list of buildings of special architectural or historic interest.

128. Chilham House, Rectory Lane, once known as Glebe Place. Mr Scatcliffe had it built in 1932-3, using timbers from an old barn at Bosham. The steps and windows on the south side were copied from the old shop at Bignor.

129.   Hardham Mill and house. The house was bombed during the last war and eventually pulled down, making way for the West Sussex Water Authority.

130.   The West Sussex Southern Water Authority works at Hardham.

31. At the time of writing there is a lot of enlargement work taking place at the Hardham water works. These huge ranes can be seen from the main road.

32. (*below left*) Beedings, known by many people as Dr. Harley's castle, is situated on a hill to the north-east f Pulborough.

33. (*below right*) Toat Monument stands on a hilltop to the left when travelling from Pulborough to Adversane.

134. (*right*) Clements Bridge after many years of use.

135. (*centre*)Clements Bridge and the railway bridge, date unknown.

136. (*below*) The old and new bridges both known as Swan Bridge.

XIV CLUBS, SOCIETIES AND ASSOCIATIONS

There is a club or activity in Pulborough for most people to join if they are interested. This chapter gives details of each one and they are listed below.

Among the most important is the British Red Cross Society which started in Pulborough before the first World War and disbanded at the end of the war. It was restarted in 1942 by Commandant Mrs. Woods who lived at the *Arun* Hotel and was a V.A.D. during the first World War. The Society has continued since that date. It is now known as the Pulborough and District Centre, District 2.

The Centre is part of the Sussex Counties Branch with headquarters at Hove. The Branch Patron is Lavinia, Duchess of Norfolk. There are about 175 members of whom 20 are V.A.D.s. This Centre covers quite a wide area and they have a caravan behind the Pulborough Village Hall which is manned by voluntary members on Monday, Wednesday and Friday mornings. They have a good reputation for money-raising which occupies a good deal of time and effort.

The Junior Red Cross consists of members from 11 to 15 years of age. They meet once a week in term time—these are the V.A.D.s of the future.

The Ambulance Station is situated at The Moat, the conveyance for the land took place in 1955 but the station was not built until 1966. There are three ambulances with ten fully-trained men.

In 1978 Mr. P. Read and his colleagues, with the help of Dr. Shillingford, started the Arun Cardiac Emergency Fund. About £25,000 has been raised since that date. This has enabled them to equip each ambulance with heart-monitoring and defibrillation machines.

In the near future a radio will be installed in each ambulance. This will give a direct link with Chichester, Worthing and King Edward VII (Midhurst) hospitals. This has been a wonderful achievement in such a short time and will be a great help to those patients who may need it.

St. John's Ambulance Brigade started in Pulborough in 1932 and registered its first ambulance in 1954. At that time it provided free ambulance and hospital services in exchange for as many hospital-stamps as residents could afford.

In 1973 a new ambulance was paid for partly by the Bonhomie Organisation and the Storrington District and Parham Nursing Association, and the rest of the money was raised by voluntary efforts. The total of £3,100 was completed by the sale of the old, original ambulance.

At the beginning of October 1972, the Pulborough Care Association held its first general meeting. This was a new group incorporating the Old People's Welfare Committee. As well as holding a meeting every three months it organises the handicrafts exhibition at the Village Hall each year.

Services for the elderly include the Wednesday Club which began in 1954 as the Darby and Joan Club. It is still flourishing with about 45 members. They meet at 2 p.m. on Wednesday afternoons in the Village Hall, the mini-bus and cars with voluntary drivers transport the disabled to and from the meetings. The 'tea-ladies', all of whom are voluntary, are there each week. This they have been doing for many years. Outings by coach are arranged for members during the summer. The Club holds a country market, enters for the handicraft exhibition, and ends each year with a special lunch.

Meals-on-wheels are a great help to the elderly and the disabled. They are delivered to about 24 people in Pulborough on four days each week by voluntary helpers who do a marvellous task in all weathers.

The community mini-bus service was started in Pulborough in 1975. It was decided to use this title because the originators envisaged it being a success and spreading and did not want to tie it down to one area. There are now five divisions, each one with its own area.

Since the early days Petworth, Billingshurst and Storrington have been covered by this service. It now extends as far as Barnham, Walberton and Aldingbourne.

The Royal British Legion was born out of the comradeship of the First World War when men lived together in the trenches. The Pulborough branch was formed in 1919 and the first post-war annual dinner was held at the *Red Lion* on Friday 27 January 1956. The branch has continued ever since and had its new standard dedicated, and the laying-up of the old one, at a special service in St. Mary's church on Sunday 15 June 1980 at 3.30 p.m. This was conducted by the Rev. Basil St. C. A. Maltin, and the Legion County Branch Chaplain, the Rev. W. P. Webb. A year pennant was added to the new standard in 1980 as 1979 had seen the Legion's Golden Jubilee; also a royal crown which the old one had lacked.

Before the service, 40 standard bearers, who were invited from Legion branches in the County, met on the recreation ground and were inspected on parade by Major General H. Lairdet, the Legion President. They then marched along London Road to the church led by the 90-strong Christ's Hospital band. After the service everyone returned to the primary school for tea. Later the band played on the recreation ground.

Members meet every Armistice Sunday, parade and attend the morning church service. After the two-minute silence a wreath is placed on the War Memorial in memory of our men who lost their lives during both wars.

The Bowling Club was, I understand, started many years ago by Mr. N. Timpkins and others. They have a well-kept green off Rectory Lane. There is also a Ladies' Section. Many times I have heard it said 'Oh! that is only an old man's game' but a lot of skill is needed to play it properly. In the past I have seen many clubs playing. A lot of young men and ladies do play and it is a fascinating game to watch.

The Cricket Club in Pulborough has been going well for many years. In the church magazine for March 1937 it states 'The annual meeting was held at the Five Bells, the Rector presiding, the club had played thirteen matches, winning seven, losing three and three drawn'.

The club is still well supported and at the time of writing an additional pavilion is about to be erected which will provide a club room, and a bar for the members.

Badminton is played in the Village Hall on Wednesday evenings. Junior members are coached by Mr. F. Hurst until 8 p.m. when the senior members take over.

The Flower Club meets in the Village Hall on the second Tuesday of each month at 7.30 p.m. Young Wives Club meets there as well on the first Tuesday of each month at 8 p.m.

The Football Club has always had a good team, well supported. I remember several years ago old Mr. Hampshire, who lived in London Road, kept everyone amused— he used to get so carried away with the game he would kick his foot right out every time the players kicked the ball. Their colours today are green and yellow. The first team is in the Premier Division, West Sussex Football League and the second team is in the Third Division, North Sussex League.

Rugby started in Pulborough in 1969. Mr. A. Mason is chairman; they now have their headquarters at the new club house. They run four sides and a junior colt side. They enter for the Sussex Cup each year and every other year they exchange visits with a French team from Fontainebleau.

Pulborough Luncheon Club, which was sponsored by the Community Care Association in January 1977, meet on the first and third Wednesday of each month in the Village Hall. This meeting is a social occasion where people who live alone can get together for an hour or so over a simple meal, which at the time of writing costs 30 pence. An average of 30 to 40 people attend.

Wednesday is the day that Pulborough has the use of the mini-bus so anyone wanting to attend and is unable to do so through disability or lack of transport can use this service to and from the Village Hall.

Boys also have their club, started at the Corn Exchange in 1947. Their No. 2 monthly magazine, dated October 1948, is quite interesting to read. It states 'There is no doubt the club has come to stay and even less doubt that its success is due largely to the unfailing efforts of our club leader'. They praise him highly and everyone joined in saying 'Thanks a lot Sid and good luck for the club's second winter season'. 'Sid' was Sid Greenfield who lived in the house in Potts Lane.

The Club appears to have had a good football and cricket season. Later it moved its headquarters to a hut in the village hall field. Some time afterwards it was renamed 'The Youth Club'. Mrs. Kelly, who was their leader for 13 years, kindly let them use the cellar of Arundale School. Now they have their own club-house which was opened in March 1977, near the new primary school. Mrs. Jill Woods, their leader, and members, worked hard to raise the money needed; one or two grants and donations were given.

On Tuesday evenings there are Bingo-sessions; on other evenings it is well used by both boys and girls. The club is most essential in a village, providing the members carry out what the club leader said in 1948—'Do remember there is a certain standard of decency, and by that standard our school, our home, and our club is judged'. He also said 'It really isn't big to destroy something of value to others'.

Several years ago the Council provided hard courts for tennis, just below the bowling green, but after a while no-one was interested so the courts just went to ruin. Today Arundale school very kindly allows people to play on their courts during the summer season. The gate is kept locked and a key can be obtained from the Head Mistress. A fee is charged, part of which is refunded when the key is returned.

About 25 Guides meet on Tuesdays, two packs of Brownies, each of about 25 girls, on Mondays and Thursdays, 25 Scouts on Wednesdays, two packs of Cubs, each of about 25 boys on Mondays and Thursdays and 20 Sea Scouts on Fridays. Meetings are held in the Scout Hut on the Village Hall Field. This building was erected in 1975 in place of the Nissen hut which had been in use since the end of the last war.

Overwhelming support for the building of a Day Centre came from a packed meeting in the Village Hall on Friday evening, 31 October 1980. A steering committee has been formed and will go into the details of the scheme. The land at the rear of the Village Hall is available and it was agreed at the meeting that the Centre should start in a small way and expand later.

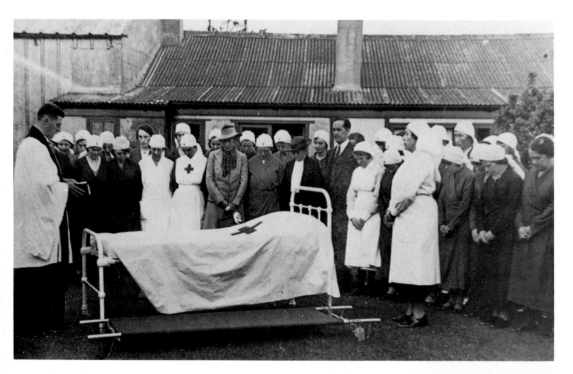

137. (*above*) This Red Cross bed was dedicated in 1939 by the Rev. Dow, in memory of Dr. Watson, their Medical Officer.

138. (*right*) A Red Cross inspection at the *Arun Hotel*, 1939, showing Mrs Watson and Mrs Woods.

139. (*opposite above*) The Ambulance Station, situated at the Moat.

140. (*opposite below*) This is a posed photograph of the ambulance men trying out their new machines. Mr P. Read, on the left, Mr B. Greenfield, on the right, and Mr E. Dunleavy, lying on the ground.

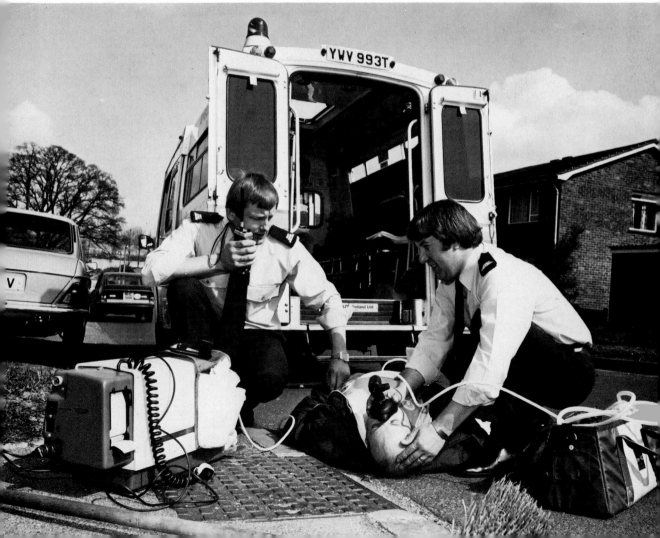

141.   St John's cadets, 1926.

142.   St John's at the May Revels, 1947.

143. St John's members, 1948.

144. Divisional Superintendent, Mr Leslie Atfield, shaking hands with Lady Louis Mountbatten at Hastings, 1964.

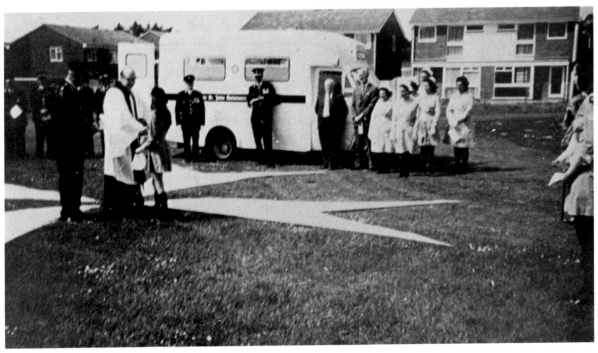

145. The dedication of the St John's new ambulance by the Rector of Pulborough, Rev. St C. A. Maltin, on Sunday 6 May 1973 at the Recreation Ground.

146. In 1929 the Royal British Legion's first standard was dedicated by the Rev. Wells of Kirdford and the Rev. T. E. Williams, assistant curate at Pulborough. Mr W. Knight was the standard bearer; with him are Mr J. Elliott and Mr S. Cranham.

147. Members of the Royal British Legion attending the Armistice Sunday service at the War Memorial, 1942.

148. Dedication of the Royal British Legion's new standard and the laying up of the old one, 15 June 1980.

149. Mr Arthur Woods carrying the new standard out of church after the service.

C. W. JARVIS,   P. G. BLACKMORE,   F. HERBERT,

M. MARSH,   A. B. BRIDGE,   W. CHEESMAN,   W. J. POTTER,   F. J. ORFORD,   J. S. OLIVER,   A. GOODSELL,   F. J. COLLIS,   W. J. BEVAN,

E. W. JOYES,   W. J. MOGER,   Rev. E. I. FROST,   H. HOLMES (Hon. Sec.),   J. B. TRIBE (President),   A. C. DEWDNEY.

150.   Pulborough Bowling Club, 1922.

151.   Some of the Bowling Club members in 1956. C. Strudwick, Mr East, J Croucher, Mr Warwick, T. Cozens, Mr Hobson, K. Peryer, E. Daley, Mr Gray, L. Hamilton, Miss D. Gocher and S. Cullen. (*Copyright Garland Collection*)

152. A Bowling Club dinner at the *Red Lion* c.1956. (*Copyright Garland Collection*)

153. Codmore Hill Cricket
Club, 1913.

154. Butler's Tea Sloshers, date unknown.

155. Present day Cricket Club, 20 October, 1980.

156. The Men's Club building in Lower Street was brought from Roffey in 1919. Mr Louis Corden started it for ex-service men and it is still well attended by these and other members.

157. Stoolball started in the Oddfellows field in the early 1920s. Club members now play on the Recreation Ground.

158. The Football team, the Red Robins, date unknown.

159. The Football team, 20 October 1980. Back row, left to right: Linesman, R. Pygate; R. Maybee;
G. Looms; L. Hookey; A. Spain; N. Pope; Front row: M. Brown; J. Leadbitter; G. Lewis; A. Leadbitter;
G. Upjohn.

160.   The Rugby team, December 1980. Back row, left to right: H. Webster; A. Steele (Capt.); A. Boyce; D. Green; J. North; D. Spencer; P. Mason; K. Langmead; S. Matanle; P. Godsmark. Front row: M. Catchpole; A. McKinnon; A. Julian; J. Stapleton; C. Shanks; J. Hall.

161.   Some of the Pulborough Scouts with Rev. Wilson Baggaley, *c.*1916.

162. Pulborough Scouts parading along Lower Street, *c.*1916.

163. Pulborough Cubs, 'Saxon' pack, on St George's Day, 1980.

164.   The Boy's Club Jumble Sale helpers, 30 October 1954. (*Copyright Garland Collection*)

165.   The new Youth Headquarters in Link Lane, which opened in March 1977.